"Mark's ability to build an authentic relationship with the athlete, as a person away from their sport, is paramount to his success. It's this relationship that forms a foundation for Mark and the athlete to truly allow for exploring and maximising the topics covered in this book"

David Willey, *England International cricketer and Captain: Northampton CCC T20 team*

"This book covers several of the most important psychological ideas tour pros will confront over their careers. More crucially, it acknowledges that a truly holistic approach to psychology is often necessary at this level, because sometimes what we do can become who we are!"

Paul Waring, *Professional Golfer and European Tour Winner*

"Working with sport psychologists before, I often found their approach quite superficial when I needed more depth, a chance to look at my identity, and ways to help both performance and personal well-being. This book covers many of the most important concepts for me in my tennis career."

Anna Brogan, *Scottish and GB Junior Girls number 1 and former WTA professional tennis player*

"Dr Nesti provides an exceptional insight into the complexity and simplicity of providing psychology support in elite level sporting environments. Drawing on his extensive experience, it is great to finally see a book that covers many of the key topics and issues I've dealt with delivering psychology in Premier League football. The text contains valuable material for anyone interested in personal flourishing and performance, and is a must read for practitioners navigating their careers in the applied world. You will enjoy the challenge of the read."

Dr. Martin Littlewood, *Associate Professor of Performance Psychology, Head of the Football Exchange: Liverpool John Moores University, UK. Formerly, First team psychologist: Leicester City, Warrington Wolves, Rangers and Aston Villa. Currently at Wolverhampton Wanderers in the Premier League*

"Whilst at the Yorkshire County Cricket Club, as well as working with individuals, Mark advised the Support staff on interdisciplinary cohesion with the well-being of players at the forefront. This was a vital component in the development of players and coaches.
I found Mark to be a man of great experience and wisdom who made a positive difference to an organization, both individually and collectively"

Martyn Moxon, *Former England cricket opening batsman, Director of Professional cricket, Yorkshire County Cricket Club*

Applied Psychology Practice in Professional Sport

Applied Psychology Practice in Professional Sport is the first text to draw directly on psychological work delivered over many years to individual players and staff inside English Premier League Football as well as other professional sports such as cricket, tennis, and golf.

A key feature of this new text is the use of examples from the author's applied practice, to demonstrate that many psychological terms and words used in the "lived world" of high-level professional sport can be understood with greater depth and meaning where these are informed by more holistic perspectives such as existential, phenomenological, transpersonal, and humanistic psychology. Implications for applied sport psychology practice are examined and recommendations offered.

Although the book is about professional sport and psychology and is key reading for those associated with this discipline, the ideas and concepts discussed should be familiar to anyone involved in supporting people in challenging performance focused environments such as business, education, or coaching professions. It is hoped that leaders, managers, and other staff from these occupations, and closely related sectors, will find the book interesting and useful.

Mark Nesti, PhD, recently retired as Associate Professor: Psychology in Sport, and MSc Sports Psychology programme head at Liverpool John Moores University. He has published seven books during his career, including the first book in the world on existential psychology and sport, an account of his organisational psychology practice inside English Premier League Football, and three books on Sport, Spirituality, Psychology, and Meaning. Formerly he worked as a Sports Council regional officer and Sports development manager and has also been an applied psychology consultant with six Premier League teams, Yorkshire County Cricket Club, and worked with hundreds of professional athletes and coaches from other sports during a 35-year career. Mark currently works as a consultant at his own company, Sportinspirit Limited, delivering psychology support to professional teams and sport performers.

Applied Psychology Practice in Professional Sport
Meeting the Person, Knowing the Athlete

Mark Nesti

NEW YORK AND LONDON

Designed cover image: Getty Images

First published 2025
by Routledge
605 Third Avenue, New York, NY 10158

and by Routledge
4 Park Square, Milton Park, Abingdon, Oxon, OX14 4RN

Routledge is an imprint of the Taylor & Francis Group, an informa business

© 2025 Mark Nesti

The right of Mark Nesti to be identified as authors of this work has been asserted in accordance with sections 77 and 78 of the Copyright, Designs and Patents Act 1988.

All rights reserved. No part of this book may be reprinted or reproduced or utilised in any form or by any electronic, mechanical, or other means, now known or hereafter invented, including photocopying and recording, or in any information storage or retrieval system, without permission in writing from the publishers.

Trademark notice: Product or corporate names may be trademarks or registered trademarks, and are used only for identification and explanation without intent to infringe.

ISBN: 978-1-032-66996-0
ISBN: 978-1-032-66995-3
ISBN: 978-1-032-66998-4

DOI: 10.4324/9781032669984

Typeset in Times New Roman
by codeMantra

In loving memory of V. B. Nesti, Father, Sportsman, Dental Surgeon, RAF Officer. 1932–2024.

Contents

Acknowledgements   *xi*

1 Introduction   1

PART I
Key psychological qualities   23

2 Courage   25
3 Belief   38
4 Passion   53
5 Flow play and happiness   64

PART II
Major existential themes   79

6 Identity and meaning   81
7 Authenticity   95
8 Spirit   103
9 Anxiety   111
10 Paradoxical leadership: learning from the best   124
   Postscript   133

Bibliography   *135*
Index   *139*

Acknowledgements

My heartfelt thanks are due to four groups of people. First, I would like to sincerely thank Megan Smith, David Varley, and Simon Whitmore at Routledge for their support and encouragement with this work. I have written several books and chapters with Routledge since 2000, and have always been impressed with their openness to new ideas, and courage to allow authors to follow less travelled paths. I do not think I exaggerate, in saying that few publishers of their standing and stature would have given me so much freedom and control over content, and the way I have tried to write. My book is very much a reflection of this refreshing publishing philosophy.

Second, to the many people, athletes and staff, of skill, integrity, and courage, I was so lucky to spend time with during the last 40 years of practice. I learned much about the psychology of professional football during my time at first team levels in the English Premier League with Bolton Wanderers, Newcastle United, Hull City, and Aston Villa. Work in professional golf and tennis helped me to grasp the different types of psychological challenges faced by individual sport participants, and recognise that many of the things experienced were common to all in high-level professional sport. Yorkshire County Cricket club provided an opportunity to work in the best, most ethically sound and professional culture, I was fortunate to experience. Doing applied work in this sport revealed constantly, that although each person must attend to their own striving for excellence and flourishing, this always takes place within a team setting where culture becomes a key ingredient.

I will resist the temptation to list the names of those from professional sport who have helped me most throughout this happy and challenging adventure. I do this, not least to avoid missing some key persons, but also in the knowledge that they know who they are, and some of them don't! I mean, that inevitably, doing the kind of personal work I was brought in to do, sometimes the most insightful, helpful, or constructively challenging support, came from those we would least expect. This list would include the kit men, kitchen staff, cleaners, and others, who can often see the real person behind the role most clearly, and possess a philosophy grounded in everyday life.

I also thank my academic mentors and close colleagues: Dr. David Sewell, Professor Andy Smith, the Psychology and Development research group and MSc sport psychology students at Liverpool JM University (2008–2019), and most especially, Dr. Martin Littlewood, a fellow traveller in the very different worlds of academia and professional sport.

Third, to those who helped me to see even more clearly how important the second group of people I have mentioned are to the development of human flourishing and performance excellence. This book therefore is also influenced by the less than professional individuals I met in professional sport. Those who assumed because you were doing lowly applied work, that you were not highly qualified, and published in the field of sport and psychology. Or again, those who resisted you because you were an outsider, the new person with little power, seen to be working in an unnecessary and esoteric area. The micro managers and control freaks, those who try to take over everything, even things they know little about, in order to alleviate their anxiety and lack of authentic identity. As in most other parts of life, people such as these also exist in high-level professional sport cultures, and so I do not think I am being unfair or unreasonable in pointing this out. They did however provide me with an unforgettable lesson. I learnt from them that character was first and foremost the real test of a person's worth, not position, expertise, or knowledge.

Fourth and finally, my wife Sarah has been alongside me throughout all of the joys, ordeals, sacrifices, and fun, of the last four decades. She held the fort when I was absent, and carried this without ever complaining about my paltry contribution to the team. Nothing I have ever written has seen the light of day without her input, as proofreader, critic, and supporter. She worked to allow me to play, to follow my vocation with her blessing. Such loyalty and support have been my inspiration. My children and grandchildren, Catherine, Vincent, Beth, Riley, and Nico. Your existence has always helped me to remember what is ultimately most important in life.

In conclusion and in more general terms, this book is based on those for whom sport has not only been a job, or offered an opportunity for a career, but also crucially, has been a personal vocation. And as the Latin roots of the word convey, vocatus is about a calling, which is the quiet voice that demands of us, that we be who we are meant to be. Something always very much easier to write than to do, but which I was fortunate to encounter in so many incredible persons I met along the way.

1 Introduction

This introduction covers theory, professional practice, and significant personal moments. In some ways it is an account of my education, one which was often unexpected and unplanned, as much as it was the result of study and formal academic development. If sometimes I appear in this book to take a strongly critical stance about academia and university life, this merely reflects my belief in the truth of G.K. Chesterton's observation over 100 years ago: Without education, we are in the horrible and deadly danger of taking educated people seriously!

On a more serious note, I would like to start by expressing gratitude to my book proposal reviewers. Amongst the many useful suggestions they made, one in particular stood out, and in some ways could be said to be a key message I would like to convey throughout my writing. In outlining what the book might cover, and the key topics and concepts to be discussed, I included little on culture and organisational environment. I suppose, on reflection, I had overlooked these areas since the focus of my earlier book on working in professional football (Nesti, 2010) had almost completely addressed itself to these matters. But what the reviewers correctly highlighted was that the way I was able to operate, the methods I could employ, and psychology I could expose my clients to was heavily influenced by the nature of the sports I was working in, and the cultures I found there. It would be very easy to claim that I delivered what I thought most appropriate and useful, and that what people wanted did not shape my activity as much as what I believed they needed. But in reality, the truth was more complex. In terms of theory, much of what has guided my work is derived from certain strands of existential phenomenological psychology. I think it is worthwhile noting what Rollo May said, that unlike most other perspectives, the existential phenomenological approach contends that the simple can only be best understood through the more complex. This is the opposite of how most normal science proceeds including psychology as a (natural) science.

In my experience no one can carry out their work, fulfil their role if you wish, in exactly the way they would like, or exactly as the books suggest, without considering the influence of the culture they are operating within. Cultures are not static entities, but are more a kind of ever changing atmosphere, where although the core principles might remain, the surface conditions are never stable. And it is with this in mind, that as a psychologist trying to help persons do better and live better, that I had to accept that not to respect each culture fully would likely result in me being unable to do the job I was invited to carry out, and eventually, maybe even lose my position! So, I again thank the reviewers for saving me from producing, if not a work of fiction, maybe even worse, a book based on an idealised fantasy. In practical terms this means that my descriptions of psychological ideas and examples of cases with real people will be coloured by the messy, wonderful, frustrating, and challenging world of elite professional sport. And for those of you hoping to come across some complex psychological words early in my book, the best way to explain what I am trying to do is captured by the German word *Lebenswelt* found in phenomenological psychology (Giorgi & Giorgi, 2008). In plain English, this word refers to *the lived world*, which describes the world we inhabit in a direct, naïve, and immediate way. It can be distinguished from, "the world of the natural scientist which is constructed or built up for explanatory purposes" (Valle & Halling, 1989: p. 9). This perspective will be a constant throughout my writing: the idea that reality is best described from how it is actually lived and encountered by real human beings rather than through the lens of abstractions and theoretical concepts.

To summarise and make things clear, the plan is to draw on psychological terms and ideas to describe my work, which should not come as a surprise since the book is officially about psychology in sport. It is just that many of the terms I include have emerged from the mouths of my clients, and not necessarily out of the textbooks on sport psychology. I hope that this focus on what athletes and coaches have actually talked about will not be seen as an obstacle, or prevent people from engaging with this work. In this, I am banking on the belief that you have picked up this book to see fresh ideas, to feel the anxiety, and even some small measure of excitement, that accompanies the discovery of something unfamiliar. In saying this, it is also my conviction that what you see will not be totally unexpected or difficult to recognise. And surely this is as it should be, if, as I am claiming, what I have articulated here is based on reality, a world directly known to us all in our everyday lives before we engage (if at all) in reflection, or any type of analytical thinking.

Another very important topic, one that seems rarely to be addressed in many books on psychology or sport psychology, is the question of ontology. I make no apologies for mentioning what might seem to be an unnecessary venture into philosophy; indeed, it might actually be more accurate to call this a question of metaphysics. Ontology is the study of *being*, in our case, *human being*: what is it, how is it constituted, and what does it mean? These are not the types of enquiries that usually appear in sport psychology sessions, although I will argue in this book that sometimes dialogue with our clients is very much about these matters if we are prepared to come at things from quite a different place. This is for later. At this point, I believe it is useful to mention ontology because it is essential to help the reader understand why and how this book has been written, and what are some of the key assumptions being made.

Well, the first is that I believe that human beings are persons; they are not objects made only of matter, whose lives are determined by external and internal forces, and neither are they pure minds, that is, subjects who are capable of creating themselves, and who possess complete freedom to do as they desire. The definition of a person guiding my work and writing is derived from what is sometimes called *realism* in philosophy. In straightforward terms, this is the idea that reality is really real! Things are not figments of our imagination but have real substance: they exist outside of our minds, and human beings have the capacity to apprehend that reality through use of their senses, body, and mind. In even more stark language, it is the common sense notion that things truly exist beyond what I may or may not think about them, and that human beings alone, amongst all creatures, have the ability to recognise and understand these things, that is, what they are and what their purpose is (despite never being able to complete this task and know all there is to know).

And whilst we are at it, and following the maxim that honesty is the best policy, I also believe that human beings, as persons, are able to think for themselves, and to make choices and decisions, because they are endowed with free will. It is this crowning glory of human being which allows us to think and act in ways that are truly ours, and which are not solely the result of our genetic inheritance, or determined by the environment. These ideas of course are not mine but are mine to share, coming as they do from two of the greatest philosophical minds of all time: Aristotle and St. Thomas Aquinas. I initially came across the work of these giants of common sense philosophy through reading a wonderful, short, but challenging book, when I was an undergraduate student. Written by the German philosopher, Josef Pieper and called, *Leisure: The basis of culture* (1963), this work introduced me to several important concepts that have guided my work over the past 40 years or so. Unfortunately, it is extremely unusual to see Pieper's insights being cited in psychology or sport literature, something I feel has had the effect of narrowing and shallowing our field in worrying ways. Examples of this would be that his writing on courage, joy, sacrifice, suffering, human spirit, and religious spirituality, meaning, hope, happiness, contemplation, and finally love, could have added greatly to our practical and theoretical work in performance psychology.

Strangely, or maybe not when I think about the history of sport psychology and psychology in the Anglo world at least, my academic writing and approach to practice have often been dismissed by some as not really psychology. The accusation is that I am essentially a philosopher, something that would make many of my professional sport clients smile after they have been subjected to one of my uncomfortable existential phenomenological psychology counselling sessions! Quite how a philosopher has been able to work inside the English Premier League and top level cricket for example, is quite a feat given the general view of philosophers is that they are uninterested in practical matters, and devote their energies to the search for wisdom (as the term *philosophia* makes clear). I believe what has happened is that because I have tried to ground my work in one of the oldest European approaches to psychology instead of North American cognitive or behavioural perspectives has caused confusion. That existential and closely related humanistic perspectives are based on a human science (Giorgi, 1970) rather than natural science footing, some, most likely due to a lack of depth and breadth of knowledge in the discipline of psychology, have made unfounded assumptions. As can be seen throughout this book, many of my references are from psychology books and articles. That some in sport psychology are unfamiliar with the work I draw on, does not justify labelling it as philosophy. You may wonder if this confusion matters, especially because my book is largely focused on applied psychology in performance domains. My feeling is that it matters greatly, because the effects of this natural science psychology dominance has in my opinion, been one of the main reasons so very few of my colleagues over this past 40 years have been able to work for sustained periods of time with the highest level of elite professional athletes and their staff. That these approaches helped me to achieve this, and have guided the work of a small number of others who work at the highest levels of professional sport is surely worthy of some critical thought and reflection. In this small group, I include friends such as the late Professor Ken Ravizza in US professional baseball, and Dr Martin Littlewood and Dr Darren Devaney at first team levels in Premiership football and rugby union.

Another contentious topic, at least for the parent discipline of psychology over the past 150 years or so, is that of values. The word value is often used in three main ways. We talk about the value of something meaning it's cost, or price. At other times, value is employed to convey worthiness; is something or someone useful, beneficial, or helpful. In recent years, value, or more exactly, *values*, has become the name we frequently give to morality and ethics. This development might be because people have become afraid to use such old fashioned and traditional language, and have instead tried to hide behind the less confrontational, bland, and obscure sounding word of values. Whatever the reason, and I feel it is partly because values sound at least more progressive and neutral than morality and ethics, there is no avoiding the fact that work with human persons is impossible to imagine without some consideration of values.

This book is most certainly not a treatise on morality and ethical codes, but it most definitely does not subscribe to the deranged post-modern notion that there are no fixed values, because there is no such thing as truth to underpin them in the first place. As an aside, it is always so amusing to point out (yet again) to the post modernists, that their idea that truth does not exist, is itself, their own truth statement! More seriously though, this book does recognise that values, that is morals and ethics, always enter into our work, how we approach it, what we think we are trying to do, and to what end. It seems to me that questions around purpose and meaning, that is, what are we hoping for when we carry out our work, are woven into all we do whether we acknowledge this or not. Psychologists and sport psychologists are therefore not merely carrying out some form of technical task and applying their knowledge in a vacuum; their beliefs about what they consider to be best ethical practice and sound moral reasoning guide their practice from start to finish.

I hope the values that guide my approach are transparent throughout this book. They have informed my choices, the cases I draw upon, and the concepts and ideas I have highlighted. It would be churlish for me to claim that I consider other moral positions and ethics as being superior to those governing my approach. That would be to fall into the post-modern trap of claiming that since we can't ever be sure that we possess the full truth or a fact about something, that truth and facts don't exist. No, such a position is duplicitous, or at least very dishonest in my opinion. Naturally I hope for, but don't expect that everyone reading this work will agree with my analysis of events, or arguments presented, but I would be disappointed if they were unable to see why I have said what I have said, or acted as I have done. After all, debate, discussion, and even disagreement are all fundamental components in any form of authentic learning; merely telling people what to think and do has never brought any success when more complex matters are at stake.

Although this is not an autobiography, in some ways it is very close to that genre. I say this because what I have done, how I do it, and why, is not only influenced by surroundings and culture, but is also my chosen way of being a psychologist in sport. It was my editorial team at Routledge who very astutely advised (instructed!) me, that I needed to include an account of my academic, professional, and even personal development, in order to explain why I carry out my vocation as I do. They were absolutely correct in requesting this information on behalf of you, the reader, since I am convinced that the psychology you espouse is no neutral venture, but often reflects closely who you are, how you view your life, and life with others. I tell my story, my unfinished story, not to convince others to follow my way, so much as to allow you to understand why I have made these choices. One of the reasons for wanting to produce this work is the hope I have that it will serve to confront each person, whether psychologists or not, with deeper questions about the psychology to which they ascribe and adhere to. After all, psychology, very much like its much older (in academic terms) sibling, philosophy, is not like physics or maths, in that it should connect to us in a very personal way. In contrast, algebra or the principles of thermodynamics, for example, are quite impersonal; they are facts no matter what we may think or feel about them. But we choose, knowingly or not, our philosophical world view and psychological beliefs. And if we are ever in doubt about this, all we need to do is ask a close friend, or better still, a family member about how they see us, our beliefs, values, and personality. They will soon let us know about these things, even if they don't draw on sophisticated academic terminology and concepts to explain them.

The start always says more than it being merely a place to begin. After all, I could commence my story from any point or perspective, but I have chosen this example, much of which remains personally meaningful, that it is still vivid to me sitting here in my home in Scotland many miles away, and over 55 years ago. I was selected, by whom I forget, to play in a county cup match with the school first 11 football team, most of whom were much older than me. I played in my favourite position on the left wing, but I probably didn't stay out there as I scored a hat trick and we won 4–1. I remember being carried off the field by these older boys on their shoulders. What joy, what delight; surely life could not be better than this ever. The three watching spectators and a couple of free range dogs at the side of the pitch meant nothing to me. I felt great helping us win, but more than this, it was the feeling that I had been me out there, just like I felt playing in the street and back garden with friends and my brothers. It all felt so normal, and despite being so nervous before the match started on the bus trip to this game, I don't remember any feeling out on the pitch until someone jumped on my back when I scored the final goal, a penalty. We were through to the next round, but in all honesty, I wasn't thinking about that. I wasn't really thinking at all, but I did feel how wonderful it was to be part of such happiness with others.

If you read the last paragraph back, you will see I talk about anxiety as a good thing, the importance of joy, and authenticity, flow, intrinsic motivation, and happiness all feature strongly. And this is some 15 years before I was to study some of these concepts at university. It seems the early seeds of my psychology in sport were being planted by the lived experience, by reality, and encounter with the real. If I remember correctly, our teacher at that time didn't do tactics, or get us to think about our mental condition. Instead, little was said, and we were left alone to play and perform guided by our love of the game, and our desire to try and do the right thing with the right spirit. Only many years later, and after formal study in psychology, did I understand that we were being encouraged to play courageously, and to draw on our intrinsic motivation towards football, or in better language, our love for the game. The seeds of performance psychology were being sown deeply into my nine year-old *being*. Learning by doing, and through dreams, thoughts, feelings, and more doing; it all felt so very natural and normal. In my work as a psychologist I would discover that almost everyone I worked with in elite professional sport had a similar tale to tell about their understanding about psychological factors in sport. Few I spoke to in almost 40 years of applied activity had radically different accounts to mine. It has always seemed to me that it is no coincidence that this group featured many world level and exceptional professional athletes and support staff. This book in many ways is their story, the data is derived from some of the very best at what they do, and is in their words, and from their lives in sport. My aim is to record their ideas and concepts, and examine them more fully and deeply so that it can help people in sport, and any other environments or activity, to flourish as human persons and improve performance. And I am quite sure that somewhat paradoxically, real lovers of sport, at any level or experience, have lived a similar psychological story.

My next existentially significant moment arose when I realised that if I was not going to be able to play sport as a job, then the very next best thing would be to be paid to think about sport for a living. And so, after losing my way over a number of years from my first love, I returned to university at almost 24 years old to commence my vocation. That might seem a rather unnecessarily strong word to use here, but I believe it is the accurate term in this context. I have always felt that what I do is not just a job, and neither is it merely my career, but instead it is truly something I feel called to do. I am quite sure that I am not alone in this, and as we have argued (Ronkainen et al., 2018), the term vocation much more closely captures the lives of many people who work in sport.

With the passion, motivation, and indeed love for what I was doing, university study, whilst a challenge as it should be, was nevertheless a wonderful four years of unalloyed joy. Educated and formed by an exceptional teaching staff, I joined a very special group of students on the Human Movement degree, the majority of whom would later on work in sport and leisure as they followed their own unique passions in the field. I was interested in all subjects we studied on our degree, but psychology attracted me more powerfully than the rest. There are likely several reasons behind this appeal, but I feel two stand out as most important. First, psychology contained within it something that helped explain why I loved sport so much. Although it would take later study to find psychology books unafraid to mention love and passion, at this point in my academic development, it was the study of motivation and personality that especially seemed to connect most clearly to why sport meant so much to me. Second, I heard top performers, coaches, and other leaders claiming that the major differences between the very best and the rest could usually be attributed to psychological factors. And more promisingly, research and testimonies from the real world confirmed that developing an athlete's psychological qualities and skills, could even help less physically or technically able individuals overtake their more gifted peers. Excited by these features of psychology, upon completion of my undergraduate degree I made the decision that I would follow a path to hopefully become a sport psychologist. I was fortunate to have several offers of PhD and postgraduate training in the UK, USA, and Canada. Eventually opting for the well regarded programme of sport psychology at the University of Alberta in Canada, I arrived with my wife just a week or so after our marriage to start the journey in earnest. I had studied motor skill learning alongside broader areas of psychology applied to sport on my undergraduate degree, and was keen to link these two disparate topics in my postgraduate research. This turned out to be much more difficult than I had anticipated. Although accepting that the study of motor control and skill learning in human movement could be researched legitimately apart from questions of motivation, personality, anxiety, and other similar psychological concepts, I expected that it would be possible to adopt a more holistic approach and look at all of these areas simultaneously in one study. Obviously, to carry out manageable research, my questions would have to be narrowed and have focus, but I felt sure that since sport is played and performed holistically, that my research could be designed with this fact in mind. I discovered that the issue was not so much about how I would carry out the research, the methods I would employ and how my results could be presented, but rested more on a philosophical view about the nature of psychology as an academic subject. In brief, the opposition to my research suggestions was more about whether psychology should only be grounded in the methods of natural sciences like physics, or if it could be related to the discipline of philosophy.

This debate sent me off to find out about the roots of academic psychology, and by extension, the sub discipline of sport psychology. I found that the dispute was unresolved in the books, but it was much more clear within universities in the English speaking world at least, that the dominant paradigm was that psychological theories and research should be seen as part of the natural sciences. This was expressed to me once, in everyday language, that for psychology to be taken seriously as a subject, psychologists had to be seen as scientists whose theories and research would be able to offer solid findings and practical solutions to problems, just like medical doctors, pharmacists, and engineers. To achieve this, so the argument went, the discipline must reject psychological theory and concepts which are not measureable, and which therefore, cannot be studied in the same way as other sciences.

Now in truth, there is much more to this dispute, ideas around subjectivity, the limits of reductionism, and control and prediction versus understanding and meaning. Fortunately, there are now many excellent accounts of this that can be found elsewhere (e.g.,Cowen, 2024: Vitz, 1997). My point in bringing this up, is that for the first time I came across some people for whom scientific purity (as they saw it), was more important than the subject, sport, we were trying to understand more fully. It felt to me then, as it does now, that people like this were not especially passionate about sport, and may even have felt embarrassed to be associated with it in academic circles. After all sport is body based, and the university is about mind and intellectualism, so maybe best not talk about it too loudly in case we were asked if we were worthy of a place in academia! On reflection, it felt more like a form of intellectual snobbery at times, instead of a calm, measured, and balanced position.

The end result for my development was that I relocated my studies with a supervisory team who at least were open to idea that sport could be studied through more holistic psychological perspectives. And very fortunately for me, at around this time I came across a book from cognitive psychologists that would provide some of the key theory for my future research studies. I had always been left a little cold by some aspects of cognitive psychology, seeing it as a kind of behaviourism but from the inside, as opposed to the strictly external focus of the behaviourists. By its own admission, the cognitive revolution in psychology developed side by side with the growth in information technology and the rise of the computer. I felt a fair amount of it seemed to make reasonable sense until it was applied to how human beings actually thought, felt, and behaved in the real world beyond research studies and the like. I could see its value in describing psychology in ways akin to computer processing, but cognitive psychology still seemed too reductive, excessively systematic, and far too neat and tidy to be able to make sense of what can often seem like the unpredictable and apparently irrational behaviour of people.

In contrast to this de-humanised cognitive psychology, the work of Deci & Ryan (1985), which they called organismic cognitive psychology, held out new promise in that it at least appeared to acknowledge that cognitions reside inside human beings, and crucially, that self-determination is an important feature of our make up. The idea of self-determination is based on the belief that our thoughts and feelings are also partly our own, and are not merely the result of the environment acting on us, or of autonomous cognitive processes that guide our behaviour. For possibly the first time studying psychology applied to sport, I had come across highly esteemed theorists and researchers who were able to accommodate the notion of human freedom, free will, and the existence of a self, even though they used more modern and scientifically sounding terms to describe this.

After exposure to Deci and Ryan's work, I subsequently took a postgraduate course in the area of personality theory because I had been told that this topic was a great way to appreciate the breadth of perspectives in psychology as a whole, and not only in the field of personality itself. I thank my supervisory team for this suggestion; they were absolutely correct, and maybe they did not realise how profound their advice had been and what effect it would have on my thinking. I remember feeling quite relieved, and even excited, when I discovered that there were a number of approaches to personality that took a very different view towards the notion of free will and freedom compared to the five most well-known personality theories of psychodynamic, neo-Freudian, behaviourism, trait, and cognitive psychology. Attracted at first to the humanistic approaches of Maslow and Rogers because of their emphasis on the centrality of personal agency in influencing our personalities, I eventually ended up at existential phenomenological psychology as this seemed more fully to relate to real life. The existential view of personality, similar to its younger sibling humanistic psychology, placed great stress on each person's role in forming their personalities, but crucially, it also had much to say on what at first glance sounded less attractive aspects of human psychology, such as meaninglessness, inauthenticity, anxiety, guilt, and loneliness. I remember being genuinely excited, that at last, I had found something in psychology which sounded so close to how I had thought about life and psychological matters before my academic education. There was the added advantage that unlike humanistic perspectives, existential psychology seemed to accept that our psychological formation involved both positive and negative features, and that there were limits to our freedom, and ability to make ourselves into anything we desire. This final element was referred to as *situated freedom*, which highlights that individual human freedom is always constrained by the environment, and by our own limitations, and responsibility to others. Nevertheless, existential psychology argues that our freedom is the most important part of our psychological make up, and that although never fully free, we do possess the freedom to make choices, to accept or reject responsibility for ourselves, and decide on courses of action. In other words, human persons are beings shaped by genes and influenced by external forces, but they are always capable of deciding how to respond to events and moments. To me, it seemed that this account was truly empirical, that is, grounded in the real, and based on the self-evident facts of everyday life, and true for all people.

I was now set free to learn more about how certain types of anxiety could be viewed as a necessary and important part of psychological life, despite anxiousness often feeling uncomfortable. That although motives and motivation were very important concepts, sometimes our thoughts and behaviour was more related to ideas around meaning and purpose. And crucially, for my later work with performers from various domains in sport, business, and education, existential psychology highlighted that rather than self-actualisation (Maslow, 1968a), authenticity was a healthier quality to pursue since this was achievable to all, and is about our freedom.

Authenticity really means to strive to be more fully yourself, to be the person you really are, rather than who others feel you should be. This task might sound like a recipe for selfishness and directed towards encouraging self-centeredness. Fortunately, some existential writers have been alert to this potential problem, and added that for your own flourishing and that of others, the journey to greater authenticity must not come at the expense of good ethics, moral behaviour, and sound values. They also recognise that full authenticity is never possible; it is achieving greater authenticity and growing in this, where we will find genuine happiness, flourishing, and our best performances.

All of the above (as we will look at in more detail in this introduction when we outline what will be covered in each chapter) provided me with psychological ideas and concepts I felt would help greatly in my applied work with athletes and other performers in the future. I was vaguely aware years ago, and this recognition grew over time, that what I had been searching for was an approach to psychology that resonated, made sense is a more accurate description really, with what I had experienced in my own life, and through participation in sport. In my journey doing applied work, I soon realised that I was not alone in seeing how relevant some of the existential themes were. And given that the majority of the people I have been fortunate to meet have often been at the highest levels of their respective sports, I knew that if what I was offering and drawing upon made little sense, these individuals would never choose to work with me beyond any initial activity. Typically, people who love what they do, and are highly proficient at it, rarely like to waste time, even to appear polite!

After returning from Canada I took the opportunity to follow my vocation outside of university life and academia, and enjoyed a very enriching period in sports development where I met administrators, managers, politicians, as well as athletes and coaches, and other sport science professionals. This experience helped confirm my thinking that psychological factors around excellence and human flourishing were not only applicable to sport participants themselves, but to everyone involved in the sport industry widely.

Renewed and refreshed, I applied and was accepted by the psychology department at the University of Hull (UK) to carry out doctoral research on the meaning of anxiety in sport. Despite being supervised by a cognitive psychologist, Dr. David Sewell, I was skilfully supported to develop my own approach to the research. This was especially important because most of my data in the next five years would be based on athletes and officials in sport who were often operating at very high levels of performance, or were professionals. Many of these individuals were, or in time became, clients in my applied practice; this was something we anticipated in our research design, and was viewed as a particular strength of the study.

During this period, the vast majority of journal articles in the peer reviewed literature focused on youth and non-professional athletes, unfortunately something which is still largely the case. Although of interest, this body of research lacked ecological validity for me since the majority of my research subjects after the first study, were older, elite, or professional sports participants.

My work was grounded in existential phenomenological psychology and its approach to anxiety. The first study used what was the main approach to the measurement of anxiety in sport, and was driven by the cognitive perspective which dominated sport psychology at this time. Collecting data using Martens' et al. (1990) Competitive Sate Anxiety Inventory (CSAI2), we found amongst other interesting results, that the item containing the term *concerned* was not always understood in the way the creators of the inventory anticipated. We found that concerned was often taken to indicate care, or being motivated, and not only worry as the CSAI2 suggested. This opened the door to my subsequent three studies which built on this finding by highlighting that the *meaning* individuals attached to anxiety differed, as much as level or intensity. Adopting a more mixed methods design, results indicated that for some athletes', anxiety was perceived positively, even if it was usually reported to *feel* very uncomfortable.

I learnt many things from my doctoral studies, but one of the most important, was that it reminded me to remember that individuals come first; their interpretation and perceptions are the cornerstone of our discipline, and that group data and results whilst useful at suggesting trends, could never capture adequately how the individual person interpreted events. I took this lesson on the sovereignty of the individual, over the group, into my applied work with both teams, and single sport performers. This philosophy of practice would not only connect well to the psychological approaches I used to guide my work, but would eventually open up some very exciting new opportunities for me.

One of these rather unexpected and happy moments, came during a presentation to applied sport psychologists about working with teams in professional and high-level sport. During the talk, I was able to draw extensively on my applied experiences to that point and PhD research, and grasped the chance to discuss some of the key elements of existential phenomenological counselling. I described the concept of encounter (Nesti, 2004), and how this term was used in existential phenomenological work to mean much more than mere dialogue between two people. I was able to discuss some case material, the importance of confidentially, the concept of Flow, and challenges associated with authenticity in professional sport team settings. I am quite sure that very few in the audience fully understood what I was talking about, since the vast majority were educated in the use of cognitive or behavioural psychology, and mental skills training (MST). I did acknowledge that although MST could be very useful, especially with less experienced or younger sport performers, that at higher levels and with older individuals', key existential issues like identity, meaning, and authenticity, frequently came up in sessions. Luckily for me, a young applied psychologist from an English Premier League Football team was in the audience. His name was Mike Forde, and the role he had involved both organisational psychology, and providing one to one support to first team players and staff. At the end of the workshop Mike came up to me, and despite knowing little about existential phenomenological psychology, asked if I might be interested in doing some work at the club. It might have been that he just liked me, my Scottish accent, or maybe some of my rather weak jokes, but he was too good a professional to allow such matters to influence his thinking. I believe that my attempts to present about how my clients often talked about issues relating to meaning, identity, boundary situations, existential anxiety, courage, self-belief, spirit, and authenticity, resonated with him even, if he might not have talked exactly about these terms in the way I did.

In the following months I was invited to meet Bolton Wanderers staff at the club, and attend a backroom staff away day. These experiences gave me an opportunity to begin to understand, how a relatively small club in terms of support and financial wealth was able to survive and thrive for many seasons in the most demanding professional football league in the world. In terms of my own practice, I discovered that access to players would be impossible without the full support and backing of the head coach. Fortunately for me, this person was Sam Allardyce, who would later go on to manage England and several other Premiership clubs, and who was well known as a forward thinking and creative individual. Big Sam (as he is known in football) embraced sports science, and was especially enthusiastic about psychology applied to football. Well ahead of its time, Bolton Wanderers had one of the largest and most highly qualified sports science and sports medicine teams in world football. Considerable effort was expended in trying to develop a holistic culture, where new scientific approaches and more traditional coaching methods and philosophies could be blended to the benefit of football performance. Described as, football in science, this environment provided the ideal backdrop for me to carry out my work. Both the head coach, Mike Forde, and the head of sports medicine, Mark Taylor, understood that performance psychology with world class Premiership footballers would only work well guided by a specific philosophy and mode of practice. The most important part of this was to recognise that building trust between the player and the psychologist would be essential, and that the best way to do this was to operate with strict confidentiality.

In practice, this meant that nothing was disclosed from meetings to any other party without the full consent of the player. The only exceptions to this would be if illegal or harmful activities were discovered, or if the player was experiencing mental ill health. These two situations would of course involve careful use of referrals, and disclosure of information only to relevant parties in the first instance. In addition, Mike and Sam strongly supported and understood the rationale behind my approach, which focused equally on the person behind the player, and the sports performer themselves. This was grounded in the principles of existential phenomenological psychology and personalist philosophy, and is based on the idea that to build relationships and develop trust, a person to person encounter would be essential. This perspective also rests on what might seem to be a common sense position, which is, that what happens in someone's broader life impacts their performance, and likewise, performance successes and failures impact individual's at a personal level.

To carry out this work consistent with phenomenological psychology, sessions involved face to face dialogue between player and psychologist. Within these encounters the player, or staff member, would be challenged to think about how they might go about improving their performances. Invariably, this dialogue revealed that common themes included dealing with coach athlete relationships, maintaining an intense performance focus consistently over a season, and not allowing one's identity to become narrowly and exclusively that of being only an elite professional footballer, or member of staff. During my first brief meeting with Big Sam, I remember him asking me what I thought would be some of the key psychological challenges that players and staff would face as performers and people. Sam and Mike, more fully, given his background in academic sport psychology, also questioned how I would be able to help individuals, and which specific areas would they need to improve or develop. Some of the content of this book is my attempt to capture the answer to those questions. The ideas and concepts I will cover, has emerged partly from my work based inside four English Premiership clubs at first team levels, but is also equally derived from engagement with elite and professional sports performers and their staff, in golf, tennis, motor racing, swimming, rugby league, and cricket, amongst others.

Before I turn to a more detailed account of the chapters contained in the book I would like to explain why, unlike most applied sport and performance psychology books, there is little mention of mental skills training (MST) or more familiar cognitive psychology constructs like motivation, confidence, stress, and arousal. The short answer is that my experience of working with mostly high-level professional performers is that they already often have excellent mental skills, and have a good understanding of the principles of motivation, the value of confidence, and coping strategies to deal with stress. In preparing this book I looked back at my case notes, client reports, and data gathered from players and staff since my first applied work in 1987, and could clearly see how little of our work together addressed psychological skills training, or topics like motivation. It is my belief that this is because of the holistic perspective I use in the approach to my work, and that so many of my clients were high-level professionals. Where I have worked with younger people at lower levels, or in an amateur context, discussion, around cognitive processes and applying mental skills training has featured more strongly.

Finally, I think it is fair to say that this book is about formation rather than education as such. That is, formation through the culture, both within an organisation, and beyond, within the broader culture of society.

More positively, our work was directed at helping the person to find their own unique and attainable way to develop greater consistency in their thoughts, feelings and behaviours.

The psychological qualities that have been described throughout this book, just like mental skills such as visualisation, or more broad constructs like motivation, must be learned, and implemented as consistently as possible. This focus on the importance of consistency, might seem at odds with the more holistic psychological qualities which I have suggested are the most important for high-level performance, and human flourishing. I think there is considerable misunderstanding that just because something is not a narrow skill or an easily defined psychological construct, that learning and improvement must take place in some obscure and mysterious fashion. The psychological qualities like courage, authenticity, and spirit can be learned by the individual through the ordinary tools we have at our disposal as human persons. In other words, studying, reading, dialogue, reflection, writing, and most importantly, putting ideas into practice in real life situations, are highly effective ways to promote change, and authentic learning. And like all human enterprises, carrying these activities out with greater consistency and perseverance is more likely to lead to the desired change.

It is important to mention that most of the examples I draw upon throughout this book, are based on some of the best people I worked with. What I mean by this, is that these were athletes or staff who were ready to embrace some form of psychology support, and who were open to working closely with me during brief, or longer periods of time. These people demonstrated courage in my view, because they were prepared to do something many people try to avoid-looking closely at themselves as persons and sport performers.

Developing self-awareness and even more counter culturally, self-knowledge, requires a number of personal qualities, of which the most important is courage. Following the definition provided by Corlett (1996a) in sport psychology, courage involves trying to do the right thing even with the knowledge that it might fail. And the right thing, as thinkers of the stature of Aristotle and Aquinas make clear, is also always a question of morality and ethics. I make no apologies for claiming therefore, that those who engaged fully and openly with the type of psychological topics mentioned in this book were invariably people of courage, since it takes this psychological and spiritual quality to be prepared to look closely at who you are, what really motivates you, what are your psychological strengths and weaknesses, and even, what is most important to you in your life.

Given the perspective that courage would be required to even begin to engage in this kind of depth psychology work, it is important to acknowledge that many individuals did not want to work with me. This group includes people from a wide range of sports and performance cultures, and represents individuals of all ages and levels of achievement. Sometimes work did not occur because of structural and logistical obstacles which made regular high quality contact difficult to achieve. For others, it was more a question of need and desire. Inevitably there are some very proficient and psychologically impressive people in high-level professional sports environments, and several felt they did not need my support, and had developed their own successful ways to deal with the psychological and spiritual demands of their role. I ensured, where possible, that all players and their support staff met with me, at least initially, to gain a more detailed understanding of how I carried out my support work, and potential benefits that could arise from this. It was always made clear that the choice to engage further was solely the responsibility of the individual concerned. I believe there is quite a sizeable group of individuals in these environments who do not need support from sport or performance psychologists most of the time, and who have acquired an extensive and impressive range of skills and psychological qualities throughout their careers. Often my interaction with these types of persons would be more oriented to me drawing on their insights about the team or group, or listening to their well-informed views around the psychological challenges typically confronting people at this level of professional sport.

I did however come across another far less admirable group of people in my work. As maybe can be easily imagined, I have not written about the experience of working with this fairly large group who did not see the value of sport psychology, or who rejected the notion that a sport psychologist could assist them in their search for improved performance or personal flourishing. I often felt that some within this particular group were afraid to engage in dialogue around psychological matters, or adopted a rather cynical perspective, doubting how someone who had not played or performed at their elevated levels of achievement, could have anything useful to offer. Again, the ideas discussed in this book also exclude those who were looking for a more superficial, or quick fix, solution to their problems and challenges.

As I will make clear in the following chapters, I am convinced that coaches especially, are best positioned to help with more straight forward, easier to action psychological advice and input. The approach I use, based as it is on dialogue within both a supportive and personally challenging framework, tends to proceed more slowly, and answers or solutions emerge more often from the person's end, albeit guided at times by my own psychological knowledge. There were also occasions often when performers faced crucial moments in their careers, that support staff, such as coaches, performance directors or medical personnel, would request short term interventions to change behaviours, or attitudes. The expectation here was that the psychologist could direct the thinking of the performer in such a way that clear, specific, and measurable changes in behaviour and performance would take place. Where I did engage in psychological work of this type, it was, in the vast majority of cases, a very small part of an overall approach based more in holistic development, longer-term work, and client informed actions.

It has to be said that sometimes my clients perceived that I was a clinical psychologist, that is someone dealing with serious and debilitating mental ill health issues. This perception of psychology, that it is a discipline aimed at 'fixing broken people', was something I encountered quite frequently from individuals with little prior experience of sport psychology, or from countries where the concept of performance psychology was little known or understood. And lastly, I did engage with players and staff who, as it became obvious during sessions, were adopting a tactical approach to our work together. By this I mean that they were only prepared to use with my services because they thought it was something that would be viewed favourably by others. For example, I vividly remember meeting in highly visible locations, such as in the communal canteen, or on the playing pitches or courts during training sessions, and being aware that the individual I was working with had chosen these environments in order to impress staff about their desire to change, and work more seriously on the psychological side of things. Although these instances could be frustrating for me, I continued to work in these less than optimal situations in the hope that more genuine work might take place at a later point. I did this work out of respect for what natural scientists refer to as the placebo effect, or as we say more usually in social sciences, the Hawthorne effect. I have always been very comfortable with the empirical fact that many good things take place, including learning new ideas, and understanding former views more fully, as a result of a person's perception and belief about what is taking place. Connected to this in reflecting on my practice over the years, I came to realise that the quality of relationship was very frequently as important as content, in bringing about any changes in thinking, feelings, and action. Not only did I see this evidence in my own work, but the best, most psychologically robust people I met, would constantly tell me that the coaching, sport science and medical staff who had the biggest impact were those who they believed cared about them as people first and foremost. In relation to this, I distinctly remember a world level performer telling me that they followed the psychological message conveyed to them by a particular member of staff, because this individual was interested in them equally as a person, and an athlete.

Finally, I hope that readers of this book will be able to recognise familiar ideas and themes, whilst others will be challenged about their own practice, and approach to psychology and performance, in whatever environment they find themselves. It is a truism that our approach chooses us, as much as we choose our approach. Especially outside of natural sciences like physics, sociologists, psychologists, and other social scientists are faced with a huge choice of perspectives, theories, and competing schools of thought from which to select their underpinning knowledge. I have long since thought that the approaches we choose and the philosophy upon which it is grounded is first and foremost a close reflection of how each of us views the world and life itself. Although this can create myopic thinking and blind spots, it is quite impossible to imagine that these choices could be made in any other way. I believe the only position that is unacceptable, and may even be dangerous, is when someone uncritically accepts a particular view or way of working, and in effect, promotes something that they themselves do not believe in, or would never accept as a guide for their own lives.

We will now look a little more closely at what each chapter will address, and how this will be done.

Courage

There are surprisingly few accounts of courage in the sport psychology literature. Recently, the related concept of resilience has received considerable interest, at least in academic circles in sport psychology and psychology more generally. Resilience and mental toughness, another recent favourite in sport psychology, are very different from the idea of courage, not least because this quality is formed in a person, and is not a skill or a technique as such.

Although few of my clients ever mentioned courage per se, their accounts of what they wanted to do, and who they wanted to be, would often reveal that they understood how central courage could be to their work and development. I will draw on a number of explicitly personalist approaches in mainstream psychology to show how courage has been considered and discussed in the discipline. From this analysis of practice and theory, I will suggest courage plays a major role in the lives of many in high-level professional sport, and that it is something we should value and nurture in sport at all levels of performance.

Belief

For almost 60 years, sport psychology research and practice have highlighted the importance of confidence. The evidence is overwhelming; high levels of confidence are usually associated with exceptional performance. One of the problems with confidence, apart from the difficulties that can be caused by over confidence, is that it tends to fluctuate strongly, and is therefore, by definition, unreliable. Arguably, a greater issue is that confidence is something we only truly feel after success (usually). This relationship is of little surprise to anyone. The real dilemma resulting from this though, is how can we perform well when not feeling confident. It is at this moment that belief, or more accurately, self-belief, is vital.

This chapter will examine why belief, rather than confidence, is the key to psychological well-being and superior performances. Examples from psychological encounters with professional sport people will reveal what building self-belief really means in practice, and why this is valued so much more than confidence.

Passion

Academic sport psychology has had very little to say about the concept of passion. Often it has been assumed that motivation and passion are really the same thing in practice, and more often than not, that passion is not something to be encouraged, and certainly not in those who want to achieve at the highest levels. Where there have been examples of articles in the peer reviewed literature on passion, these most usually describe passion as a problem in sport, and as something detrimental to enjoyment and performance.

My experiences from the lived world of professional sport have given me a different point of view about the benefits and drawbacks of being passionate. This chapter will draw on holistic and philosophically informed psychological approaches, to argue that passion has the potential to be a positive in sport. Through use of reflections on my applied work, I will discuss how passion, defined as "love accompanied by suffering" has much to commend it in sport, and other areas of life where performance is important.

Flow play and happiness

Happiness and sport; this is a phrase that might be expected from a book on recreational sport and play, rather than one on high level and professional sport. In this chapter, I will draw on accounts of happiness from humanistic and phenomenological psychology which have enabled me to make sense of how this term can be experienced in the lived world of professional sport. Arguably, the nearest concept to happiness in psychology literature is Flow. Derived from phenomenological research in mainstream psychology over 50 years ago by Csikszentmihalyi (1975), the concept of Flow has been applied to help understand performance in a wide range of human activities, including sport. Phenomenological psychology can be quite a complex idea, and is certainly very different from most other approaches in academic psychology. Phenomenology has the advantage of being close to common sense notions, at least around the question of how psychologists should go about getting their data, and how this can be discussed. Finally, I will discuss how Flow theory can help us understand more about the relationship between play, happiness and performance in the lives of those who play professional sport. Descriptions from individual sessions carried out with staff and athletes will also be considered. I will suggest that the concept of play could be especially fruitful in helping us discover more about the relationship between participation, performance, and happiness, for all who take part in this sport, no matter their level, or ability.

Part II of the book focuses on four of the most important topics in existential and other personalist approaches in psychology.

Identity and meaning

Although the concept of identity has been considered in sport psychology literature for a number of years, the dominant approach has tended to focus on the topic of athletic identity. Research based on this conceptualisation has been useful in warning about the dangers, especially to youth athletes, of developing a foreclosed athletic identity. Largely missing from this work on identity has been an awareness of other, more holistic perspectives, although recently there have been some important attempts to take a broader view, linking this concept to meaning, purpose, and spirituality.

This chapter will build on these perspectives and examine how identity is experienced in the lives of professional athletes and support staff. Examples from practice will be used to reveal that identity is a key element in psychological well-being and performance success, and is something high-level professional sports people focus on, and seek to develop, throughout their lives.

In relation to identity, the notion of meaning, or life purpose, may appear to be something that individuals' in professional sport might only begin to consider as they leave sport. There has been some attention devoted to this concept in the literature on transition and career termination in sport, although rarely has there been much discussion about meaning itself, but rather on the need to find new meaning.

Based on individual psychological work with hundreds of professional athletes and staff, I will examine how questions around meaning or life's purpose emerge much more frequently than might be imagined. It is my belief based on these applied engagements, that feelings of meaninglessness, and the need to commit to something which gives sense to life, is a common feature in the lives of many in professional sport. I will draw on psychological approaches and psychologists who have placed the need for meaning as a central element of human well-being and flourishing, and discuss how this topic can be dealt with in sessions with professional sport performers.

Phenomenological and existential ideas will feature strongly in this chapter, partly because according to Maslow (1968b), these were the first perspectives in psychology to emphasise that questions around identity are central to psychological, emotional, and spiritual health, and flourishing.

Authenticity

Very simply put, the idea of authenticity in psychological terms refers to the notion of trying to be more fully who you are meant to be. This might sound quite a straightforward task, however, there is much clinical and research evidence that this is not the case. In my work with professional sports people, the struggle to be less inauthentic and more "fully themselves", was a constant theme, not least during the challenging periods when performance levels dropped, or where the easiest thing to do was settle for the quiet life and merge into the crowd. I will argue that some strands of existential psychology have much that could help applied practitioners grasp why authenticity is such an important concept, and how we can help our clients attain this more fully, and more often. Giving examples from players and staff at different stages of their careers in professional sport, this chapter will hopefully begin to reveal why greater authenticity can be an aid to both psychological well-being, and performance, in professional sport. Recommendations will be made about how sport psychologists, and others, can guide their dialogue in encounters with clients to support them in their desire to become less inauthentic, so that the real person, the one they are meant to be, can appear more frequently, in good times and bad.

Spirit

The rationale for including this term in the book is first and foremost, that this word is frequently mentioned by staff and athletes in professional sport. Within my applied sessions, ideas around spirit, spirited performances, and the spiritual have often emerged. Sometimes this has been in relation to the importance of religious spirituality and belief in the lives of my clients; at other times, it has been more about human spirit, and terms like courage, sacrifice, joy, and love. There has been growing interest and some impressive literature on the topic of spirituality and sport during the last 15 years especially. I will draw on some of this work, and my own insights and experiences, to describe how ideas around spirituality could help us understand high-level professional sport more fully. I will also give examples of ways in which dialogue with athletes and staff has touched upon this topic, and helped their personal well-being, and professional performance.

Anxiety

As one of the most studied concepts in psychology and sport psychology, anxiety has a long history in terms of research and applied practice. Typically, anxiety has been viewed in quite narrow terms as something related to competition, and usually as a negative feature of sport performance. This chapter will follow a very different path in considering how anxiety can be viewed as a beneficial experience, and indeed, that it is something high-level professional staff and athletes often welcome, and see positively. During applied sessions, I regularly came across accounts of anxiety which were at odds with most of the traditional sport psychology literature on the topic. I will look at how using broader, more holistic approaches, like existential and phenomenological psychology, can throw a new light on anxiety in sport, and allow it to be understood as something which frequently accompanies learning and growth.

Anxiety has been confused at times with excitement. Part of this reflects the psychological approaches used to guide research, such as cognitive and behavioural perspectives, where the emphasis is on how something appears, or is felt, and thought about. In contrast, existential phenomenological psychology commences from the real lived experience of the person, and focuses more on meaning. For example, someone might say I think that I am very excited by what is about to take place, and also feel somewhat anxious about it. In everyday language this might be expressed by something like, "I can't wait to do this, but I really hope it goes well though". A closer analysis would reveal that the first part of this sentence describes a sense of excitement, looking forward with joy, whilst the final part mentions hope, which could be interpreted as being aware that the experience might not go as well, or be as enjoyable, as planned.

Dialogue from fully confidential encounters with my professional clients will be used to show how specific types and levels of anxiety were accepted, and even welcomed, as indicators that optimally demanding challenges were being sought and experienced.

Paradoxical leadership

Although this book is not primarily about leaders or the concept of leadership in professional sport, I feel it is important to say something about this topic because of the importance of culture. Leaders, in whatever capacity, have a big part to play in building and developing the performance culture. This chapter is based on my observations of the personal psychological qualities of the leaders I encountered. I have also included another list which is more focused on the conditions and psychological atmosphere found in the best cultures. I believe it is within these types of cultures that teams, and individual persons are most likely to acquire and grow the psychological qualities discussed in Chapters 2–9. Finally, many of the ideas are expressed in the form of paradoxical statements, since I believe these capture the picture more fully and accurately.

A special note on persons

Within the following work, I have tried where possible, to use the word, persons, rather than individuals, clients, or subjects. Many psychologists follow what could be termed as personalist approaches; the best known are humanistic, existential, and phenomenological psychology; Jungian perspectives could also arguably fall into this camp. The definition of what constitutes a person is therefore a very important feature in how I carry out my work, and it shapes my understanding of human health, flourishing, and excellence.

Although the account below is derived from a Catholic Christian meta-model of the person, I believe much of what is says might be shared by other psychological and philosophical perspectives. The model draws on theological and philosophical ideas, but has been developed specifically for the psychological sciences, counselling, and mental health practice. Devised by Titus et al. (2020), I believe it is a complex, and yet immediately recognisable, account of personhood.

As an aside, it is worth recalling that Rainer Martens (1979) reminded the fledgling discipline of sports psychology to always attend to the person first, and the athlete second. It seems to me that some of what he was saying was to stress the importance of the dignity of the human being over their role or function. Unfortunately, Martens' very important seminal article did not provide a definition of the human person, possibly seeing this as something beyond the bounds of psychology. As a result, since that time, with the exception of my own very basic work (Nesti, 2007a), and that of Watson (2011), few in sports psychology have had had much to say about the concept of person, preferring instead to talk about participants, clients, or individuals in their work.

The discussion that follows throughout this book can really only be fully understood in light of the definition of the person provided by Titus et al., however, there are many other religious, philosophical, and even psychological perspectives, where similar ideas are found. Titus and colleague's definition includes reference to theological and spiritual ideas, and I would recommend that people access their more complete account. In describing the human person Titus et al. state that

> the human person in an embodied individual who is intelligent, uses language, and exercises limited free-will. The person is fundamentally interpersonal, experiences and expresses emotions, and has sensor-perceptual-cognitive capacities to be in contact with reality. All of these characteristics are possible because of the unity of the body and unique self-consciousness, and are expressed in behavior and mental life. Furthermore the person is called by human nature to flourishing through virtuous behavior and transcendent growth; through interpersonal commitments to family, friends, and others; and through work, service, and meaningful leisure. From their origins (natural and transcendent), all persons have intrinsic goodness, dignity, and worth. In the course of life, though suffering from many natural, personal, and social disorders and conditions, persons hope for healing, meaning, and flourishing.
> (p. 5)

What follows within this book therefore, is very clearly grounded in a specific account of the what it means to be called a human person.

Part I
Key psychological qualities

2 Courage

Although few of my clients ever mentioned courage per se, their accounts of what they wanted to do, and who they wanted to be, would often reveal that they understood how central courage could be to their work and development. I will draw on a number of explicitly personalist approaches in mainstream psychology to show how courage has been considered and discussed in the discipline. From this analysis of practice and theory, I will suggest courage plays a major role in the lives of many in high level professional sport, and that it is something we should value and nurture in sport at all levels of performance.

Maybe one of the most surprising features in relation to courage is how rarely this concept has been discussed in academic books in psychology, or sport psychology. This might seem all the more remarkable because this word is used so frequently by politicians, journalists, military personnel, those involved in healthcare, and of course, by the general public. In addition, it does not take too long to find coaches, sports leaders, and athletes mentioning courage, especially when they are talking about return from injury, performing against the odds, and trying to do the right thing in difficult circumstances. I always wondered what lay behind the absence, or near absence, of reference to courage in the academic subject of psychology. It is not as though the parent discipline of philosophy has ignored this important quality of human persons. Aristotle, as one of the giants of philosophy amongst other things, and Aquinas in the early Middle Ages, as well as other more contemporary philosophers like Heidegger and Nietzsche, devoted considerable effort at defining courage, and suggesting why it was so important. In more recent times, philosopher Josef Pieper held that courage was the most important virtue, although he pointed out, *that courage does not exclude fear*. Along similar lines, existential psychologist Rollo May stated many times, that for human persons, *being is never given automatically, as it is in plants and animals, but depends upon the individual's courage; and without courage one loses being.*

And with this very brief introduction, I believe that it is quite easy to deduce why most of psychology, since its formal founding in the mid-nineteenth century, has usually avoided any reference to the concept of courage. This has occurred largely as a result of psychology, especially the type that has come to dominate university teaching and research, as well as, somewhat paradoxically, much of therapeutic and applied psychology, being grounded in reductionism. The reductionist perspective,

DOI: 10.4324/9781032669984-3

derived from philosophical materialism, has tended to uncritically copy the approaches and methods of the natural sciences, especially physics. We have touched on this problem for psychology, and by extension, sports psychology, in the introduction, and it is a constant theme throughout most of this book. It seems as though in an effort to gain scientific respectability, to be able to measure, quantify, and predict, psychology has been prepared to abandon its earliest roots. And despite what appears to be a common misconception, psychology did not start with the experimental work of Wundt in the nineteenth century, and neither was Freud the first to draw on psychological ideas to help people. Psychological concepts like courage were studied and discussed when psychological ideas were considered part of philosophy, usually in a branch known as moral philosophy. That the modern study of human psychology has restricted itself, almost universally, to concepts that fit neatly into a natural science paradigm has, I am convinced, undermined the credibility of the discipline instead of strengthening it.

Fortunately, however, in the real world this scientific and methodological purity counts for very little. This empirical fact is ultimately my overriding reason for including a chapter on courage in the book, and because the concept of courage was frequently alluded to, either directly or indirectly, by most of the professional athletes and support staff I worked with. Of course, given the complexity of this term, there were moments during dialogue, or listening to sports professionals talking to one another, that I felt it necessary to check carefully that what they were referring to was truly courage, rather than other closely related notions. One of the ways I will pick up on this issue will be by looking more closely at differences between courage and bravery, and compare this term with the more familiar psychology and sport psychology constructs of resilience, and mental toughness. In terms of developing more courage, the case study example will describe some of the ways in which a person can build courage; hopefully, this will clarify how different the human quality of courage is to mental toughness and resilience in particular.

One of the most impressive articles I ever came across in the sport literature was by Professor John Corlett. His paper was provocatively titled, *Courage in sport; virtue lost* (1996b). In addressing the specifically Western account of what constitutes courage, Corlett made two very important points, particularly when applied to professional practice. First of all, he pointed out that courage is always and everywhere, a matter for the person themselves. Although we may talk about a courageous group of individuals, he argued that this phrase can lead to a misunderstanding. For a thing to be fully and genuinely courage, it has to emanate from the individual person themselves, and be something that they have chosen, rather than being acquired as a result of collective action, or the decision of others. And even more contentiously, but with huge practical implications in sport and other areas of life, a courageous act, to be called such, always involves a moral and ethical component. We will look in more detail about what this definition of courage means for all human persons, and specifically consider some of the implications of this in professional performance sport environments.

I belive that it is impossible to write meaningfully about courage in any applied sense without referring to choice, freedom, and anxiety. The psychologists' who have brought the greatest clarity on the relationships between these terms have usually been those who are wholly, or partly, guided by the principles of existential phenomenological psychology. By considering their work in more depth, I hope to show that courage is not a mental skill that can be acquired once and for all; to be switched on and off as the person sees fit. Instead, by drawing on this existential psychology body of academic literature, and my own applied engagements, I hope to convince others that courage is a human quality formed and chosen over time, and through exposure to a certain culture and environment.

The examples in the chapter are largely drawn from professional golf, tennis, and cricket. This is quite deliberate and reflects the highly individual nature of these sports, albeit that cricket is played in a team format.

One of the most interesting ideas around courage is contained in the scholarly work of the existential psychologist, Rollo May. His book, *The Courage to Create* (1975), explains how the creative process depends to a large extent on a type of courage. The ability to be creative, to produce innovative and inventive solutions to challenges, is important in all areas of life, but especially so when trying to develop new approaches and ideas. In this sense we can speak about the courage of great scientists, artists, and inventors, who often took what was a lonely and isolated position, and provided new insights and fresh perspectives. In sport, at all levels, but most especially where athletes are highly skilled and possess outstanding abilities, teams and individuals will often look for creativity to break down opponents and seek an advantage. Being creative by definition comes with risk, because the process involves not so much novelty itself, as doing, or thinking about something, in a unique way. The risk of course is that this might not be the best solution having never been tried before in exactly that way, and could lead to poorer outcomes and even outright failure. We will look at how sports performers in sessions with me tried to increase their capacity to be creative, despite the feelings of anxiety and self-doubt that accompanied this. At these moments, it would sometimes be very clear that in order to try to be more creative, the person realised that they needed to think, or act, more courageously.

And finally, attention will be directed at looking briefly at why courage is sometimes necessary to help the individual not to do something. The idea, often confused with the closely associated concept of bravery, seems to have arisen that being courageous must always involve a positive movement. The reality is that there are many times in all areas of life, including in high level professional sport, where courage is shown by not engaging in certain behaviours, or thinking. We will look at why this is often a much harder enterprise for people to follow. Given what is at stake in professional sport environments, there is a tendency at times for people to feel that more of something is always better. I hope to explain how in practice, the much harder thought that, less is more, or inactivity is best, can sometimes be the most courageous position to adopt.

Vignette on courage: staff example

In this case, a relatively inexperienced new member of the sports science team came across some important information and feedback from a number of overseas players. This related to their perception around how physical fitness data was collated and used by the sports science and coaching team. The young sports scientist arranged to meet with the club psychologist to discuss the issue in more detail and consider a way forward. During this meeting it became clear that the sport scientist was very concerned about their own ability to accurately explain the problem to other more senior members of the backroom staff. Despite being convinced that the athlete's concerns were very legitimate, and indeed could actually be used to improve practice throughout the club, the sports scientist was anxious about being seen as taking the player's side and being perceived as weak. They explained their understanding of the issue to the psychologist. It seemed there were a number of problems, especially around how the data was perceived by coaches and shared amongst the group. It was felt that instead of helping athletes to improve individually in terms of a range of physical fitness parameters, data, either deliberately or not, was being used to embarrass athletes and contribute to unhealthy division within the playing group. The sports scientist explained how the athlete had made what he considered to be several very helpful suggestions about better methods of using the data, which would not undermine motivation and could be viewed more constructively. The decision was made to call a multi-disciplinary team meeting to enable the young sports scientist to bring this matter up for discussion and resolution. Prior to this event, the sport scientist met once again with the sports psychologist to rehearse their arguments and outline the points they planned to present. On the morning of the meeting, the sport psychologist received a phone call from the sports scientist, who said that they now felt very unsure about the meeting, and thought the best action would be to avoid bringing this topic to the attention of other staff members. During dialogue with the sport psychologist, the sports scientist expressed how incredibly anxious they felt about taking this action, and they speculated on how it could undermine trust and relationships, especially with the head of department and other key staff. After lengthy discussion about their feelings and thoughts around the issue itself, the sports scientist decided that they would go ahead with the planned meeting, and provide the feedback as intended, because they knew that this was important, and the right thing to do. Later that day, the sports psychologist was able to catch up with the sports scientist to ask how things had gone in the meeting. They described that they were so nervous to begin with that their mouth was dry and they could sense their heart beating much more strongly than usual. However, once they began to explain the player's perceptions, and propose the solutions they had suggested with advice from the sports scientist, the reaction from the group, after being initially very defensive, became highly supportive. Over lunch time, several players had approached the sports scientist to ask how the meeting had gone, since he had told them that this had been scheduled for early morning. They were impressed and delighted that he had shown the courage to bring these ideas forward despite being the least experienced and newest member of the staff team. Before leaving the training ground, the sports scientist was called into a brief meeting with the head of department. They were commended on having the courage to carry out such a potentially difficult and delicate task, especially given that their appointment to the role had not been universally supported since not only did they lack experience, but that their previous involvement in professional sport was at a much lower level. The head of department complimented them and stated that despite being aware of some of their limitations, he had been very keen to employ them in this position, because he could sense that they possessed considerable courage, that is the capacity to try to do the right thing, even in the face of great difficulties and obstacles, and possible failure.

Courage is not bravery

The first thing to say, is that all of the most important writers on courage have made it clear that it is not the same as bravery. In some ways this is quite unfortunate, because it is commonplace in much of everyday life, and I would argue even more so in professional and performance sport, to hear these two words, bravery and courage, being used interchangeably.

Maybe one of the most powerful ways to begin to explain the difference is to state that cheating can never be associated with the concept of courage. The athlete who deliberately engages in foul play, breaks rules knowingly, or seeks other ways to gain an unfair advantage, can never be described as courageous. Although these types of actions might involve some level of physical bravery, they do not qualify as courage. To be courage, we must attempt to do the right thing even though there is a chance that we may fail. And as Aristotle, Aquinas, May, and others have explained, the right thing means according to morally appropriate behaviour and thoughts. If we look a little closer at what constitutes courageous thinking and acting, the best definitions are in agreement that this must involve a moral decision at which an attempt is made to do something on behalf of another, and to base this on truth and goodness. This of course opens up a whole new debate about the concept of truth and what constitutes goodness in human being. This discussion is not primarily my concern at this moment, although I would hope interested readers will look carefully at the work of moral philosophers and theologians who have tried to find answers to these questions. But to return to the lived world of sport, an example might be more instructive in teasing out the difference between courage and bravery, and why to be courage, something must be grounded in a very specific moral perspective.

I once came across a highly respected and experienced head coach who told me in no uncertain terms, that bravery was common place in professional sport, but that courage was more rarely found. When I listened to his attempt to separate these two concepts in practice, amongst various things he said, was the idea that bravery should be seen as something that is more instinctual than courage, almost a type of spontaneous behaviour which any person would be expected to show. To make his position more vivid, he described how physical bravery, especially where we react to physical threat or challenges, was something no professional athlete could do without. On the other hand, courage was the name he gave to something that has been considered, thought about, and crucially, where there is time to decide what to do. The example might be where a professional athlete deliberately chose to carry out some action that hopefully could benefit the team's performance, but which came at great risk to their own success. In cricket, for example, this might involve a player continually trying to put themselves in the line of fire against a fast bowler in order to help a younger or less experienced player. In other words, in order to help the team effort, or in this case their playing partner, they have decided to place themselves in harm's way, which could result in physical injury or a short innings, and failure to score many runs. This courageous action by the batter might last for a day or more in the field of play, and of course, it could be that it is all over after one good delivery from the bowler. But if this was carried out as a choice by the individual, to help others, and at risk to themselves, then this would constitute an authentically courageous act. Most likely, especially if the courageous athlete remained in the field for many hours, journalists, media, and other commentators would likely herald this as an example of great bravery, and selfless action. There is no great problem with this confusion of terms until, and if, this misunderstanding infects our thinking in the practice of sport.

Especially in the more physically demanding sports, it is quite common to hear coaches, journalists and fans, equate courage with physical bravery. This is quite understandable because it is self-evident that in boxing, rugby, and other similar contact sports, a high degree of physical bravery is required to be able to complete many of the tasks and skills. Even in these types of extremely physical and potentially dangerous sports, it is still possible to see how bravery and courage diverge. If we take the example of choosing to play these games in the first place, assuming that decision is made freely and by the person themselves, will involve some level of courage. This is because, as we have already discussed, courage to be courage must involve a personal decision to do, or not do, something. In simple terms we can say that it takes to courage to choose to take part in an activity that could lead to serious injury or worse. I have seen this type of courage amongst professional cricketers, rugby and football players, where although they had chosen these sports many years before, they still had to take the field and face up to the very real possibility that they might get physically hurt or injured.

Courageous character

When people talk about the potential for sport to build character, I believe that one of the key qualities they have in mind is that of courage. It has been said many times before that sport itself is less good at developing character, and is more capable of revealing someone's character. Despite this, interest in the character formation potential of sport has a long history both in practice and in theory. And even without the voluminous writings on this matter, some of which are very excellent and arguably much needed, it is not hard to recognise that the type of sport we have, the ethos that governs it, the morality and ethical codes which guide it, will be key to what type of character this human activity can help develop.

In my dialogue with high level professional athletes, I was always incredibly impressed and excited to listen to them talking about the importance of courage in their lives on the field of play and beyond. Often expressed in terms of wanting to do the right thing, even if this came at great cost to themselves, their goals, and achievements. Tennis players and golfers would tell me stories of how they would try to fulfil their talent for the sport by continuing to play, train, and perform, even when this came at great cost to them financially, socially, and psychologically. Although it may sound very strange to our ears, these athletes spoke about the battle they had with themselves as often being the hardest to face. Especially during times where they were travelling the world to play events, making life harder for the families left behind, experiencing precarious financial situations, and maybe not making the cut, or losing early in tournaments, the temptation was to retire or leave the sport. During these moments, they would talk about their need to consciously choose again and again to follow a difficult path to try to fulfil their passion, and love for their sport. It sounded as though the courage involved here was much more personal and was about the athlete trying to be true to their calling, and confront their authentic self. But the level of discomfort, sacrifice, and even suffering that was experienced along the path, convinced me that what they were doing was building a character of courage. Many times we would talk about the moral choice of leading such a focused, and at times, selfish looking life, in order to pursue their dreams. This weighed on their minds, and for the best, courageous decisions to continue always included this moral dimension. They were aware that their achievements always owed as much to the support of other people, as their own efforts.

Courage and mental toughness

If we look at the example below it becomes clear that courage has very little to do with the newly popular idea of mental toughness. Research has been carried out in sport psychology to identify the factors associated with mental toughness, which inevitably has led to the development of psychometrics to measure levels of this construct. The impetus for this work could have come from the fact that leaders, especially in performance environments and sport more specifically, have always talked about how essential it is that people possess mental toughness to be able to deal with setbacks and adversity. In asking what they meant by mental toughness, my own experience with coaches and other leaders is that they were usually very clear. Mental toughness was the everyday non-technical term they used, to describe the ability of someone to persist with a task, even when facing great obstacles and challenges. This has always seemed to me to be a reasonable account, and I feel so much confusion and waste of energy could have been avoided, if we had left things at this. Although initially there may have been some scope for research to examine the range factors relating to mental toughness, this construct has unfortunately become viewed by some as something that can be taught like any other mental skill. And if we can teach it, we can measure it, or so the story goes. I also believe it has served to distract some in sport psychology, and psychology more generally, from considering the concept of courage.

In terms of key differences, those with high levels of mental toughness are expected to persist strongly on the task in hand; in contrast, a person exhibiting courage might actually decide to disengage from a task, or might try to carry it out in a way that actually makes it more difficult to achieve. For example, a courageous act on the field of play might see an athlete try to keep performing when according to the rules, they could take a medical time out, or toilet break. This action may actually make the achievement of their goal, which is to play well and win, even harder to attain. Again, we might see a coach or leader deciding not to appeal for a decision they are entitled to according to the rules, and which could help their team, where they believe that they would gain an unfair advantage. Courage, to be courage, is always informed by a moral decision as these two examples show. Mental toughness does not have to include this important element.

Another example from practice reveals a further important difference between courage and mental toughness. There are times when the most courageous act is to refuse to do something, or withdraw from the task. This idea can be applied to all human life, and equally to our thoughts, words, and behaviours. This might be a reason why courageous activity is often missed in the moment, and only becomes easier to see and understand over time. That someone or something can be misjudged or worse as not being courageous, is yet more evidence of how difficult it is for us to be courageous. It is no mere play on words to say that sometimes being courageous requires courage, not least because a truly courageous thought, word, or act might be denigrated as cowardice, at least until the broader context is revealed.

Courage and resilience

Courage is more associated with the currently very popular term of resilience. When we describe a person as being resilient, I think it means that they are capable of withstanding shocks to the system. In more psychological terminology, these individuals are better able to cope with stress and anxiety, and are able to react in positive ways when facing these challenges. Maybe the best way to see the construct of resilience is to envisage it as being a part of the concept of courage. There are, I believe, two ways to describe this. First, courageous people need to be resilient, if this means to personally be able to thrive and succeed when experiencing a wide variety of stressors. Second, being courageous always means to try to say or do the morally best thing, even if this could cause great hardship or difficulties for the person. In this way, we could argue that someone without resilience, or who has little of this quality, is much less likely to be courageous. It is important to remember though, that every human person is capable of being courageous, even those with little resilience, since to be or think courageously does not entirely depend on our psychological make up and abilities, but is truly more connected to our spiritual selves. A more complete account of this relationship between psychology, courage, and spirituality can be found in Chapter 8. At this point, it is instructive to note that the athletes and staff I engaged with who were considered the most courageous in thought, word, and deed, were very often those with an active religious belief, or who possessed, as the coaches would say, "*a great and generous spirit*".

The moral dimension which is a fundamental element of the courageous thought or act, has important implications when applied to practical situations in sport. In stark terms, the individual who deliberately breaks rules to gain an unfair advantage, or who with their full awareness engages in cheating, foul play, or violent acts, is not expressing the psychological quality of courage. In recent years there seems to have become a blurring of categories, and what are otherwise expressions of cowardice are confused as some form of courageous acts. Although accepting that some level of physical bravery might be involved in deliberate fouling or violent play, for example, these acts are everywhere and always a sign of cowardice. We can say this, because in contrast to courage, the coward employs unjust means to attempt to achieve their desired aim. I came across an important large minority of people, both athletes and their support staff, who desired to be as courageous as they could in all that they did. Usually, this was expressed by the simple but incredibly powerful term of wanting to be someone respected for doing the right thing, even if this came at the expense of achievement and success. During these moments of dialogue, I would feel very privileged and humbled to listen to individuals working in highly pressured and stridently achievement oriented environments, talking about how important it was for them to be these types of people. Quite often, and without any prompting from me, athletes especially would talk about other performers who they wished to emulate in regard to this psychological quality. They described in great detail their understanding that trying to be more courageous in all that they did might bring temporary setbacks, and even cause conflict with their peers, coaches, and others. They also knew that it would be very difficult, and most likely misperceived as a form of self-righteousness, to express these views publicly and in the media. Ultimately, when asked what was the main reason for wanting to play and perform more courageously, and avoid the weakness of cowardice, they would refer to the need to be able to respect themselves. A closer inspection of what this form of self-respect meant in this context, would reveal that the person wanted to do as much as they could to be congruent with the moral and ethical codes guiding their lives. And very often, they would explain that this meant in every part of their life, as a professional sports performer, and in their life outside of this. On occasions we might then talk about specific ideas around morality and ethics, and I believe as a consequence of working with practically oriented people, exemplars of people they wished to emulate in relation to courage would be identified. Interestingly, these examples of moral courage would often come from very different sports to their own, or could often relate to people from history, or life situations outside the world of professional sport.

I do not think however, that courage in the face of physical danger is the most important quality that managers and coaches are looking for in their players. A bit like the earlier discussion about bravery being expected and common place amongst professional athletes, physical courage is not usually seen as something worthy of exceptional praise. In my experience, there is another form of courage, which can throw more light on the psychological and spiritual quality of courage. And this form of courage is usually lauded, and seen as something very special. I mean the courage shown by the person who is prepared to try to do the right thing even when they have previously failed, or may likely fail again. In practical terms, this could be where a football player continues to demand the ball even when they are having a very bad game, or when the creative midfielder continues to look for the game breaking pass even though it could easily result in failure. These and many other examples from team and individual sports, on and off the field of play, are valued highly in professional sport since they can help performance and bring success. And of course they can also lead to failure and defeat, and some of the responsibility for this will rest with the courageous athlete who kept trying to do the right thing, in the right way, but who did not succeed on the task in the end. This final observation is another reason why courage is so valued in high level professional sport; the courageous act in always first and foremost something done at the level of the individual person. This does not mean that a team cannot display courage, but to do so is only possible because of individual decisions and action. Collective courage can only mean this if we attend closely to the best definitions of this quality. Group courage always means the combined effect of the courage of each person.

Vignette: courageous athlete

As a sports psychologist especially in professional cricket and top level football, I frequently worked with players who had joined the club from other countries with very different traditions and cultures. One of my tasks was to meet these individuals as early as possible during their time with the club. Drawing on existential, phenomenological, and personalist approaches in psychology, dialogue was always aimed at understanding the athlete as a person and as a professional player. In practice, this meant that much of the time could be taken up with matters which so called life style advisors tend to focus on. Of course, as a psychologist, my focus was not on broader life issues in themselves, but how these directly or indirectly affected the player's performance. Against this background, players would discuss domestic arrangements for their family, and more narrow concerns around opening bank accounts, accessing medical services, education, and availability of places to pursue their religious faith. In addition to this, and usually from people who the club had proactively sought out, dialogue would focus on the expectations that they had, and what they perceived the staff expected of them. On one occasion, a highly experienced international player who had been over a month at the club expressed how frustrated they had become about the type of role they were expected to adopt. They had been recruited after the scouting team at the club convinced the head coach that the player would be able to easily adapt to a new position for them on the field of play, because they had watched them perform well in this role at their previous club. Unfortunately, what had not been considered was that the standard of competition in their home country league was very far short of the new environment they had joined. The assumption was that as a world class player, this person would be able to come to a new country, one with a very different culture and approach to their sport, and produce their usual high level. In working with the player during this difficult critical moment, the sport psychologist helped them to clarify the options they had to allow them to meet more closely the expectations of the head coach and other staff. After several sessions, covering narrow performance related matters and broader life issues, the player chose to arrange a meeting with the head coach to explain why they felt unable to carry out the role they had been given, and to suggest how best they felt they should be used to help the team and their own performances. The player also knew that this choice might leave them facing a very difficult situation; ask to play in their preferred position, or seek to leave the club. The pressure on them was extremely intense, not least as they were the first person from their country to play for this club and in this league. Again, agents, most of their family and friends advised strongly against organizing a meeting with the head coach to attempt to resolve the problem they faced. Despite this well intentioned advice, the player felt committed to going ahead with the meeting. They described that this made them feel very isolated and anxious, and wondered if the choice could be avoided, and to see if things might improve on their own over time. In the end the player agreed to meet the head coach and explained their views and proposed solutions. This took great courage, and was something that the head coach, as a former player themselves, fully understood from their own lived experience in the sport. The end result of the discussion was that within two months, the athlete was placed on the transfer list, and moved to another club at a lower level of performance in a different country.

Acquiring courage

I have seen some excellent practices in professional sports clubs, especially, where the coaching staff deliberately created conditions aimed at developing courage in young players. Sometimes the approach involved placing young athletes in very challenging situations and environments. Often these were based on traditions of building character through adversity. Players might have to carry out arduous tasks, and sacrifice their own goals and achievements to help others. I saw staff deliberately allow athletes space and time to take responsibility for their actions, to choose how they wanted to address a challenge, and be left alone to reflect on what they had, or had not done. It seemed that the best staff were attempting to create the type of anxiety that existential psychology describes as a good if uncomfortable psychological experience. This psychological approach views some kinds of anxiety as being closely connected to the concept of courage. This is explained in terms of the feeling that accompanies the thought that we must try to do something, something we care about and want to do well, but that we might not achieve our goal. In a sense this can be seen ultimately as being about a battle with oneself, with the desire to try to do the right thing, and do it well, despite there being a very good chance of failure.

There is no doubt that people have the ability to learn from these experiences, and in so doing, begin to grow in the quality of courage. I witnessed the best coaches and other staff helping this process by asking their athletes to think about how they thought, felt, and acted, during these challenging moments. This would allow them to understand more fully that although courage is always based on the real actions of the individual person, it can be formed, deepened and made more truly part of someone's psychological and spiritual make up through the help of others. And especially with the work I saw in individual sports like golf and tennis, and the cricket skills of bowling and batting, players were constantly striving to make things difficult for themselves in training and practice sessions, to be able to face moments of adversity when in the heat of match play, and competition. This was sometimes about improving the capacity to deliver high level skills under the heightened stress and anxiety that can surround top level professional sport performances. What I saw as a psychologist seemed often to be about much more than testing and improving physical, technical, and psychological skills, important thought these are. In my dialogue with athletes it became clear that much of the time they were trying to build what has always been referred to in the rather broad term of character. Drilling down into this concept by looking at detailed descriptions of what the athletes thought they would improve, as well as why it was so important to them, led me to believe that courage was the key ingredient they hoped to acquire and grow.

I feel that both the athletes, and those who support, guide, and help them from a variety of specialisms and disciplines in professional sport, are often very reluctant to talk explicitly about courage. I think this has a little to do with it being seen as an old fashioned term, and maybe one that has military connotations, or at least, that cannot be used in what is after all, a form of play, no matter how elevated the level. In my view, this is a very unfortunate mistake since courage is so essential to performance in all areas of life, including professional sport, and just because a word is no longer fashionable, is no reason to forget it still exists. And to make matters worse, this general reluctance to talk about courage, to make clear reference to it in our training and development programmes with athletes, has opened the door to the idea that resilience or mental toughness, *as skills to be learned*, are all we need. Being a resilient person may, or may not, be a psychologically healthy thing. There are, as in all walks of life, individuals who are resilient, that is deal effectively with adversity, but who are engaged in harmful actions, and immoral or unethical behaviour. Again on similar lines, we can have mentally tough criminals, or within a sport contest, those who cheat, infringe the rules, or refuse to play in the spirit of the game. If being mentally tough means the morally neutral idea of *being able to keep going when the sensible option is to give up*, then obviously it could apply to the most wonderful of human actions, as well as the worst. In addition, the accounts of mental toughness and resilience that prevail in much of psychology and sport psychology, are based on the idea that since these are mere skills, they can be taught, acquired, and learned, much as we could do with any other skill. And it is here that we find the concept of courage is so very different. Courage, in contrast, always involves the moral and ethical element of trying to do the right thing. And even more devastating for our increasingly quick fix addicted modern culture of the easy way, courage, since it is not a skill but a personal psychological and spiritual quality, takes great effort and time to develop, and can never be acquired fully.

3 Belief

In this chapter I want to examine more closely why belief, or more accurately, self-belief, is prized so highly. The majority of books on sport or performance psychology contain chapters on confidence, and during the past 50 years, a huge number of articles have been published in scientific journals about confidence in sport, and why it matters so much. If we stop and think for a moment about this phenomenon, it should come as no surprise to understand why this concept has been written about and studied so extensively. We all know from personal experience that good performances often take place when we are feeling confident, and conversely, that a lack of confidence can lead to poorer outcomes, and even outright failure. Again, if we move away from the academic literature, we are very familiar with top level performers recounting how valuable high levels of confidence are in helping to achieve outstanding performances. I have always felt rather perplexed as to why we have spent so long investigating the confidence performance relationship when it is so well understood, and has been experienced by most of us at one time or another. It seems to me that the more interesting question could have been around over confidence, why this happens, what it means, and how to prevent it, if at all. There might also be scope to look at belief differently, as captured in the somewhat paradoxical statement attributed to John Henry Newman, *that belief implies that we hold a level of unbelief as well.* An even more challenging idea about the concept of belief from the spiritual writer, Thomas Merton, could have very practical implications for how we try to build self-belief. He has claimed that to become myself, *I must cease to be what I always thought I wanted to be, and in order to find myself, I must go out of myself, and in order to live I have to die.*

In my applied work with elite professional athletes and their support staff, I was impressed frequently by their recognition that confidence was ultimately of less importance than self-belief. I intend to look more fully at this perspective in the remainder of the chapter, and also provide examples of how such an important psychological quality can be attained and nurtured.

Finally, in thinking about the reasons as to why confidence has been so much more the focus of study and interest, I have the following observations to make. Becoming more confident has always sounded to me like a psychological skill, something an individual could acquire through a more or less rational process, and systematic program. I remember coming across a number of interventions which

DOI: 10.4324/9781032669984-4

promised the participant an increase in confidence upon completion of their training. My initial reaction, followed over the years by on the ground experience and critical reflection, was that somehow, it all sounded too good to be true. It seemed that confidence could apparently grow and increase by assimilating a number of impersonal and objective requirements. For example, we might be told to only focus on past successes, to remind oneself that they possessed the skills necessary for the task in hand, and that to remember you had successfully faced similar challenges before. These ideas in themselves make sense psychologically speaking, but that was not the source of my objection. The real difficulty for me was that the person was being led to imagine that they could somehow develop the skill of confidence away from the heat of the battle.

In my dealings with so many elite performers, I also became aware that they distrusted the idea of acquiring the skill of confidence prior to an event. This was forcefully explained to me by opening batters in professional cricket, and penalty takers in professional football, who recounted that nothing could prepare them psychologically to deal with the stress and anxiety of their roles except by going through the experience again and again. I think they were right to describe this as part of the way they developed belief, something that crucially could help them achieve success no matter how confident they felt.

My second concern around confidence was that there seemed to be a misunderstanding that many of the very best always felt highly confident before a difficult challenge. In fact, in my dialogue with these persons, it often appeared that they were so anxious not to allow overconfidence to appear, that they artificially suppressed their feelings of confidence before they went out on the course, court, or playing field. I remember asking how often they felt very confident before important performances, and given their exceptional talents, I think I was a little surprised to hear that this was a rare occurrence. Conversely, my encounters with them suggested that a lack of confidence was often the more prevalent thought and feeling. This psychological condition might be more easy to understand if we remember that defeat and failure are the overriding experience for most. Recently, there has been a rather lovely interview doing the rounds on the internet where one of the world's greatest ever football defenders, Paulo Maldini, claimed that he had been a great failure. His evidence to support this statement, is because he lost in the finals of more major trophies than he won. I think the point he might be making, is that everyone, even the very best, experience loss, and failure at some time, and as a result, it is impossible to always feel confident prior to an event. At less celebrated levels, the empirical fact is that most professional athletes and their support staff are visited by failure and defeat, more often than victory and success, over their careers. It is my conviction that they are able to keep working, and trying to follow this challenging path, because they do not rely on the impermanent feeling of confidence, but rather, are ready to return to the fray, fully committed, even after much failure, because of their self-belief.

As a final word on this brief introduction, I think it is of vital importance in psychology and related social sciences, that great care is taken to identify the precise meaning of words. This becomes all the more important where terms are often used, in practice if not in theory, in an interchangeable way. I feel this is especially important with confidence and belief. Although these two words and concepts quite clearly share a similar root, given that both are about feelings of competence and affirmation, they are nevertheless quite distinct and specific. Confidence is something which has a transitory nature; it comes and goes, often very quickly, and is most strongly linked to successful recent previous performances. In contrast, belief has a more permanent quality, and is largely impervious to what has just taken place. Belief of this type does not reside in a transient moment or temporary success, but is instead the result of a deeper lasting quality which is grounded in the totality of a person's experience, successes, including near misses, and failures.

Confidence and belief

After over 40 years working alongside coaches and high level professional athletes across many sports, I have listened to discussions about why confidence is not belief after all, because confidence is fragile and ever changing, whereas belief has a feeling of permanence. And as I have often heard, it is negative or unhelpful beliefs that are often more of a problem, than the presence or absence of confidence. Lacking in belief, or more correctly we should say, self-belief, is a much greater obstacle to overcome, because this quality is best developed and nourished by the person themselves. It is notorious that if a person has low levels of self-belief, even the best coaching, leadership, and culture, cannot grow this without the active participation of the athlete themselves.

To return to the question about why confidence has often been described as belief and vice versa, we need to look a little deeper at how these words are used in practice. The question of why this has become something that is apparently readily accepted, especially by some who occupy positions in academic settings, will cast light on how this state of affairs has arisen. I believe that there has developed a tendency, which is now more of an orthodoxy, to reject the idea that words should describe reality, that is, the truth, or facts. Living as we do in a post-modern universe, one that has been for the most part promoted by the universities, there seems to be less of an appetite to say what we mean, and mean what we say. The argument goes that if truth does not exist independently of what I say it to be, then why should we get worked up about the precise and exact meaning of words? New terms are forever appearing, language is described as fluid and organic, and therefore surely words, likewise, can change their meaning. Against this backcloth, it is easier to see how words like confidence and belief have morphed to mean the same thing.

Self-belief

As I have alluded to in the previous paragraph, belief is often mentioned alongside the more psychological sounding term of self-belief. We hear coaches, leaders, athletes, and teachers, constantly talking about ways to build self-belief.

Self-belief is usually taken to mean trusting in ourselves. This is a pretty basic definition, and at first glance, it appears quite uncontroversial. After all, if human beings possess some measure of freedom, then surely it is a very healthy thing to believe in yourself. But we know that this more philosophical account is not what people usually have in mind when they talk about self-belief. And it is this area that I want to turn to now, since I think that it throws much light on some of the problems we see with this in professional sport.

"If you don't believe in yourself", as the saying goes, "then how can you expect others to"! At first glance this seems a very reasonable point of view. In fact, if we are honest, it sounds to be even more than this, in that it comes across as a very healthy and positive position to adopt. After all, psychology has taught us that thinking well of ourselves is an important part of mental health and well-being, and that our thoughts about what we can achieve, are very often more influential than the opinions others hold about us.

Unfortunately, for some, the term self-belief has increasingly been used as a type of camouflage, one which hides a damaging truth beneath. The reality is that on occasion, having strong self-belief does not indicate a healthy outlook about the importance of human agency and freedom (as it should); instead, it has degenerated into belief that the self is fully autonomous. I will argue that this development has taken place largely without our knowledge, understanding, or even consent.

In one of his usual pithy and brilliant paradoxical statements, Chesterton pointed out that believing in yourself is quite natural, since it is only another way of claiming you exist. He went on to say however, that the person who *only* believes in himself is quite dangerous, and uses a colorful example, in pointing out, that the mental asylums of his time, were notorious for being full of people who only believed in themselves! In a further explanation, Chesterton proposes that the real problem is that those who claim only to believe in themselves, often appeared to be unsure even about their own existence. He describes this as a type of madness which possessed some of the most educated people of his time, who despite being convinced of their own selves, viewed all life as a meaningless collision of random particles and atoms.

In a sport context, especially in applied settings, it is very common to hear sport psychologists and coaches telling athletes that they need to have greater belief in themselves. At one level this is very easy to understand. It has been pointed out earlier in this chapter that over a career in sport, most professional athletes will experience defeat and loss many more times than victory and winning. One of the psychological effects of this experience is that confidence and self-belief can be undermined. There is ample anecdotal evidence and research to support the idea that performance anxiety increases as confidence and self-belief decrease. And apart from being an uncomfortable emotion, this type of anxiety tends to interfere negatively with performance. This experience is easy to understand, indeed, it is so obvious, that it does raise the question as to why so much money and time has been devoted to researching something that very few people are not familiar with, both in competitive sport, and elsewhere.

Another way to look at this topic, is to ask what we mean when we say that someone has lots of self-belief. In our usual way of speaking like this, if asked what self-belief actually means, we might describe it as being a conviction, simultaneously thought and felt, that we trust ourselves. If we persisted with the line of questioning, and asked who or what the trust was directed at, we might be told it is about the task we are facing. Not fully satisfied with this answer, a further enquiry could reveal that trust, in more precise terms, means that we are quite sure that the skills and abilities we possess, are the real source of our trust. In other words, we have reduced ourselves to something we feel we have complete autonomy over, and which it is in our power to use in each new situation we face. Now it is my contention that if we re read this line of reasoning we will come face to face with two striking contradictions. The first is that self-belief can sometimes refer to belief in things that are not in fact us, ourselves, but are more about things we possess as persons, our abilities and skills. This way of talking is so familiar to us that it is very easy to overlook that in this type of self-belief, the self has ceased to exist. Instead, we have been reduced to what we have, and not who we are. This has echoes of the warnings from Abraham Maslow and the humanistic psychology movement. They tried to reorient psychology and modern life, at least in the West, to focus more on being, than having. Unfortunately, despite what Maslow may have intended, humanistic psychology became associated with approaches that stressed the importance of the self over anything else. Self-actualization, which Maslow seems to have meant to be about seeking ways to fulfil our potential, *our being*, has become for some, a call to the pursuit of self-gratification and *having* at all costs. The unfortunate consequence of this is that for some the Self becomes our master, and great efforts are turned inwards, in the belief that satisfying its demands, will lead to perfect fulfilment and happiness.

The other noteworthy aspect is that we are now solely defined by our inherited abilities, and what we have managed to acquire by our skills. No room exists for luck, fortune, or fate. Even more problematic, everything becomes centered on self, on the individual and their accomplishments. The idea of community as an integral part of self was diminished, and has been lost to a great extent. Ironically, it appears that the self-proclaimed era of personal discovery, peace, and contentment has ushered in a period of narrow self-interest and excessive individualism. This excessive focus on the self has been identified as a major factor in the breakdown of community life, and undermining of the common good, which appears to be happening in many places.

The effect of these trends on psychology, and the psychology of sport have been just as great as in other areas of life. It has long been standard advice in coaching manuals and sport psychology literature to recommend that all should be done to help athletes develop greater levels of confidence and self-belief. Now at first glance, this seems to be a fairly uncontroversial stance. The problem with this perspective however, is that it serves to turn things upside down. To help us see why this is, it is necessary to remind ourselves about one of the most important justifications for sport.

Although disputed by many sports sociologists and historians, especially those who subscribe to progressive and liberal interpretations of society, it has been commonly felt that sport has the potential to form a particular character type, or a set of psychological qualities and personal virtues, as I would prefer to say. That this ideal guided how sport was to be established and played, can be deduced from the activity of many of the greatest civilizations of the world. To give one example, what unites sport in ancient Greece and Rome, the medieval world, Victorian times, and up to the present day, is a belief that this type of human activity, by its very nature, has the potential develop courage. And arguably, a key aspect of courage is that it becomes a crucial part of our psychological make up at those moments when we lack confidence, or self-belief. We have looked more comprehensively at courage and its relationship to psychology and professional sport in Chapter 2, but it is worth re iterating that courage allows a person to act in the absence of confidence or self-belief, and therefore, is an incredibly important psychological and spiritual quality for someone to possess.

If we return to considering the self, it can be understood as representing the totality of our psychological, emotional, social, and spiritual identity. From a specifically phenomenological psychology point of view, the self allows us to refer to ourselves as, myself. Strange as this might sound, without a self we can't identify others as not being myself. The self allows us to recognise that we exist as distinct, unique, and individual entities, ultimately apart from others, and therefore with our own identities, and freedom to act as we see fit. Some philosophers refer to this quality of the person as agency; this is the idea that human being's possess the capacity for independent thought and action, and as a consequence, what they think and feel, say and do, is not solely the result of instinct or environmental forces. Such a positive view of human freedom, based in human reality, allows that we have some say in the formation of our self, and its influence on us.

Now if this all appears to be a little too academic and metaphysical even, I would like to stress that seeing the self as something we can shape and influence has been of immense value in my applied work with high level performers in a range of domains, including professional sport. If self-belief means to believe in oneself, then first of all we need to know what it is we think we are believing in. Or to express this in plainer language: if you don't know yourself, how will you be able to believe in yourself, especially in situations when no one else seems to. The very best I have worked with, which by the way does not always mean those at the highest levels in terms of success or external achievements, these people are strongly aware of their self, its strengths, and weaknesses, failings and greatness. And what is very often true, they know that their self is always incomplete, never a perfect and finished entity as it were, and must ultimately be grounded in something larger than itself if it is to remain humble, open to new knowledge and ideas, and retain its dynamism.

Practical self-belief

In the everyday language of the professional sports coaches I have listened to throughout my applied practice, I have often heard them encouraging their athletes and support staff to, "back themselves"! Usually this phrase is uttered during periods where individual, or team, confidence levels are low. This could be returning to play after a serious injury, or having been out of the team, or not playing at this level of performance for quite some time. In a team, it could be after a run of bad results, and poor performances. I would suggest that most of us can easily recognise this, and that these are not difficult ideas to understand from a psychological point of view. Like most language from the *lebenswelt* (i.e. the lived world, the world of reality, rather than that of theoretical concepts and abstraction), there is great psychological depth and insight that can be mined from the use of this term at these particular moments. First of all, I believe that these athletes and coaches were reminding each other that when confidence is absent or low, and doubt alongside negative anxiety fills the air, the most influential psychological factor in future success will be the degree to which the person possesses self-belief. I would be an incredibly wealthy individual if I had a pound for every time I heard the sentence, that, the very best, are the very best, at backing themselves in the most difficult of circumstances. Whilst the word, "backing" could easily be translated in this context to mean deep commitment, the inclusion of the self presents a more complex picture.

In dialogue with my clients, I often discovered that the content of their self was frequently made up of three interrelated elements. One of these was about their values, the moral and ethical codes they relied on to guide their thinking and behaviour. Another area was their memory of success and achievement when facing similar challenging moments. Finally, and somewhat paradoxically, their self was partly a reflection of how others viewed them. Within my confidential counselling sessions, performers would often be very detailed in terms of identifying which others views they considered most important, why this was, and how this helped them. Although not in all cases, it seemed that the most important external contributors to their self were individuals whose values aligned with their own, and whose judgement and experiences they rated highly. Typically, these important voices would amount to no more than three or four people, and often included those who had known the athlete through moments of considerable adversity, as well as successes. In talking about why they held these people in such high esteem, it was possible to hear the person describing the values, psychological qualities, and sometimes psychological skills, that they admired and wanted to develop in their own selves. This type of dialogue, as can be seen from the example below, gave me the opportunity to ask the client about which of these psychological qualities, skills, and values, they believed they possessed, and which they hoped to strengthen, or acquire.

Some of the most important moments to build the content of the self, emerge from the most arduous and dispiriting phases of life. It seemed that at these very difficult times, that the well-known saying, *in times of danger the rescuing force grows stronger*, often became a reality. Athletes, coaches, and leaders, would describe how they felt that it was only when they reached rock bottom, when they imagined that they could not continue, that it was as if a huge burden had been lifted from them. Often, quite suddenly, they felt hope, and had a sense that all was not lost, and that it was now more clear than ever about what they needed to think about, and try to do. As could be imagined, the suggested course of action was as wide ranging and as unique as the individuals themselves, and the situations they faced. I would try hard at these moments not to suggest possible courses of action or propose solutions, but encourage the person to struggle through their own thinking and identify authentic ways to respond. I am convinced that my role in these sessions, no matter how frustrating and even exhausting at times, was to support the person to follow this process, and to resist offering my own ideas on the specifics of what they should do. For authentic, genuine learning to take place, we must walk just ahead of our client to guide the process, but be shoulder to shoulder as they consider, reflect, and eventually decide on a specific course of action.

Finally, the self, and therefore the core of self-belief, can be strengthened by critical thinking about the experiences someone has been through. This huge pool of data from the lived world of the person, will contain within it, thoughts and feelings which are often left untapped, and can easily be obscured by normal life. Helping the client to revisit this, and make sense of what they remember can be an essential task in helping to build self-belief. In this work, I always felt that my input should be a little more active, and that I should help the person to clarify and understand some of their experiences from different perspectives to maybe their usual way of seeing them. It is at this juncture that either within the dialogue, or in written form after the sessions, I might connect some of their experiences to psychological ideas drawn from existential, phenomenological, or spiritual psychology.

What existential psychology refers to as *boundary situations*, that is moments where we face a personally significant and important change in our lives, are often the occasion for the building of self-belief. For example, boundary situations could be around the professional athlete failing to get another contract, being seriously injured, or sold to another club against their will. More positively, it might involve being chosen for a national team, moving up to a much higher level of competition, or securing their first professional contract. It is easy to imagine that in certain situations, these experiences could force the person to re-evaluate their lives, to consider what is most important to them, and who they are. This final question about identity can lead to thoughts about many things, including deep and honest reflection on the content of their self-belief. In my sessions, I have often worked alongside persons during these boundary situations, and encouraged them to articulate in their own words, what they believe they are good at, and identify the evidence for these beliefs. I have found, that in general, the more experienced the person is in their chosen profession and vocation, the easier this task becomes. I am convinced this is because they possess years of hard evidence from their past of what they are able to do, and what they have achieved. The next task is to help them to use these thoughts and the accompanying feelings, to remind themselves of what they know they really are capable of, despite being in a situation where they are facing new challenges, possibly for the first time.

Vignette: building self-belief

The athlete had recently made the transition from youth level into the professional ranks. I had met with them over a period of two years, and we had developed a good relationship. The focus of the work was often on managing their broader life outside of sport, and becoming more self-aware around how they reacted psychologically to the situations they faced on a daily basis, and in competitions.

The coaching staff had expected that this player, would, in their words, "absolutely fly" in the first team environment, largely because they saw him as such a highly confident person. The reality was quite different. After almost a year in the first team squad, the player had fallen back in their performances to such a degree that the staff were now considering not renewing their contract for next season. I remember in one session he talked at length on how his confidence as an athlete, and as a person, had vanished largely, and that he was now dreading each day at the club. I took the opportunity to get him to look more closely at confidence, at why he felt this was so essential, and how it could be improved. As I had listened to many times before, the athlete explained that confidence came from doing well, and that without good performances and results, their confidence would remain at an all-time low. They mentioned how they believed, that with just one of two good performances, feelings of confidence would return, but that this was unlikely to happen now because of how poorly they were playing. In other words, they were facing the frustrating scenario, that performances would be unlikely to improve without feeling confident first, but that confidence could not be found without good performances first!

I remember the despairing look on their face when they realised that confidence was not going to appear, no matter how many books they read on the topic, or how much they thought about it. This was a great opportunity to talk meaningfully about self-belief, and about why this psychological quality, and not confidence, was the most important for them to develop in order to have a long, and successful career, at this level of professional sport. The easiest way I found to do this, was to ask the athlete if they thought that the best players they knew were always confident. They replied that they knew, and what's more, could actually see sometimes, that they were not, and yet despite a lack of confidence, these individuals still managed to perform and do well. I then probed a little more, and challenged them to explain how this could happen. The answer I heard summed things up perfectly: "I suppose it's because they really believe in themselves, even if they are in a tough patch performance wise, and this allows them to still do good and great work, despite not feeling that confident".

We next looked at the concept of self-belief, what it was, and how could it be developed and strengthened. I remember being delighted, although I tried not to show it too much, when the athlete said, I suppose it is really about me believing in myself first, as without this, I will never fully benefit from the belief others have in me.

We then began the process of looking carefully at the reasons that would help him to believe in himself more fully. Together, we talked about what they knew they really did well, and how they had produced excellent work earlier in their career despite not feeling confident. Our dialogue then turned to the importance of reflecting on this, and reminding himself about this, especially before training and competitions.

Excessive self-belief

We are quite familiar with the idea of over confidence, and the poor outcomes that can often come from this. That it is so well known, and such an obvious issue, might be one of the reasons there is so little mention of this topic in academic sport and performance psychology literature. I believe however, that there is another, more concerning, explanation behind this lack of interest in the idea of excessive confidence, and this is less easy to defend. Put simply, selling the idea that keeping confidence levels in check is a vital psychological tool to acquire is a much less appealing message to sell. Much easier is to convince people that various techniques and methods can be quickly learned to help build and develop greater confidence.

If we look at self-belief, it seems that in general, there is considerable interest in developing this psychological quality with younger people especially. I believe that this heightened desire to build self-belief has emerged in recent years, at least in Western countries, as a reaction against what was perceived to be a more critical, less forgiving, and harsh philosophy in education, training, and coaching in the past. In very basic terms, it was believed that results and performances were often affected negatively because teachers, coaches, parents, and employers, undermined people's confidence, and relied more on coercion and threats to achieve results.

Although there may be some merit in this view, I feel it has been greatly exaggerated, and has caused, or at least contributed to, a number of very unfortunate psychological outcomes. One of these, it seems to me, is that in order to shore up self-belief, we may have given people too much self-belief, and made it harder for them to accept that their failures might be due to lack of ability, poor skills, or insufficient effort. Although not exactly the same psychological concept, the notion of self-esteem has been treated in a similar way during the last 60 or so, years. The psychologist most associated with this concept, Martin Seligman, has gone so far as to say that we have largely misunderstood his work, and that self-esteem should be based on what we achieve, no matter how modest. In other words, the work comes first, and self-esteem follows, and it is this quality, arsing in this way, that we should then recognise and celebrate in all persons. Building self-esteem in isolation from actual achievements, has, in Seligman's opinion, probably done more harm than good (Seligman & Csikszentmihalyi, 2000). It might also have reduced the happiness and enjoyment that comes from feeling good about doing a difficult thing well.

In summary, over confidence and excessive self-esteem are terms rarely discussed in most books in psychology, unless these are drawing on personalist, existential, and phenomenological accounts. But out in the real world, where feelings are often secondary to actual achievements, my experience told me that many people are very aware of the problems associated with over confidence, misplaced self-esteem, and our concern here, excessive self-belief.

When a person comes to realise that they still have important areas to address, to assimilate and learn, progress can be made and development take place. I often found that some of the top performers I worked with, began to see their self-belief in quite a radically different way at these occasions. They would talk about how fortunate they were to have been born with the skills and qualities they possessed, even though they also acknowledged that they played an essential role in improving these, and using them in practical situations. In my reading, especially with the work of Josef Pieper around human authenticity and love, I began to see that these athletes and support staff accepted that they had been lucky to have been born with exceptional abilities, and the opportunity to develop these. The awareness that they had done nothing to merit these gifts, I believe, contributed to the high levels of humility these persons possessed frequently. And humility is without doubt, one of the most essential psychological and spiritual qualities to have. Humility helps prevent that brittle and rigid form of total self-belief, we sometimes call arrogance.

Humility is not something that can be learned like a skill, or by reading and study. And additionally, as the old joke goes, it is not possible to say, I believe through my hard work, efforts, and abilities, I have become a very humble person! This is because it is more correct to say that humility is formed, not taught, or acquired after patient analysis and debate. This quality grows in a person who has learned through experience and critical reflection, that personal knowledge, skills, aptitudes, and abilities, are never complete, or fully perfect. Humility is that psychological and spiritual quality of being aware that we will always fall short. It also reminds us that we need help from those around us, good fortune, and constant effort to be, and do better. This idea of humility is similar to what we hear about in the major religious traditions of the world. This is especially the case where adherents are reminded that only God knows all and is perfect, and therefore the task of the person is to accept that their achievements are the result of their own work, *and* the abilities which have been bestowed on them from their creator.

I have often felt that the most impressive people I worked with had learned the lesson of humility, and its liberating, and powerful effect. Sometimes this understanding only emerged after having been overly confident, or possessing unshakeable and complete self-belief. These performers had, as we all do, encountered adversity in their personal or professional lives, and found that they did not actually have all the personal resources, be they psychological, intellectual, emotional, or physical, to deal successfully with these challenging moments. As high achievers, this self-knowledge usually came to each person as a great surprise, and after trying hard to resolve the issue with their own capabilities.

Strangely, the new found levels of humility after these events, appeared to me in dialogue with these people to have actually strengthened their self-belief, and most certainly helped them to be more aware of the talents they *did* have, and where they were lacking. In this way, I found that some of the most humble persons I worked with, were very often those with the most robust and resilient self-belief. This finding is remarkably similar a very thought provoking study by the late Mihalyi Csikszentmihalyi, published in 1988. His research revealed that the most able people in his sample of top business CEOs, NBA basketball players, and other high achieving individuals, rated highly on two apparently opposite qualities at the same time. For example, he found these individuals were strongest in both humility and self-belief, most ruthless and compassionate, and goal oriented yet highly creative.

It is as though these pairings helped prevent dangerously extreme expressions of each quality.

We will now look at an example of how an excess of humility can actually lead to great personal and professional difficulties.

Vignette: the case of too much humility

It is very common in high level professional sport, to discover that most of the coaches, sports scientists, and other support staff, did not achieve the same levels of playing performance as the athletes' they are working with. This can bring many advantages, although one of the drawbacks can be that staff might feel at times that they are somehow not as good as the people they are trying to help and guide. This can be related to something known as, imposter syndrome, which is the feeling of inadequacy that can arise when working with people who have greatly surpassed your own previous attainment levels. In professional sport, I noticed that this occasionally had the effect of reducing the likelihood a coach or other member of staff would challenge an athlete, or suggest a new approach, even where they believed this was necessary.

One such case involved a very experienced and proficient member of the support staff. I had worked with them for several years on how they could deal better with the psychological demands of their role. As is frequently experienced in organisations with a large support staff, conflict and disagreements can take place about the best way to deal with players, and which approaches are most beneficial. This person was being repeatedly undermined by two others, one their superior, and another who was at the same level, but from a different scientific discipline. Their interference and extreme criticism of the work philosophy and practice of my client had led him to consider leaving his post, and moving out of professional sport altogether.

In our confidential one to one sessions, we looked carefully at what actions could be taken to help address the problem, and how these could be carried out. Dialogue and follow up reports revealed that a number of choices had been carefully thought through, and the best way forward decided upon. And yet repeatedly, despite such good work taking place in our sessions around some very difficult and complicated matters, he would fail to follow through on his ideas in practice. Looking more closely at this avoidance, we both could see that he was struggling with excessive humility and a lack of self-belief. He explained that he often felt so lucky just to be in the building and being able to work with such exceptional people, both staff and players, that he often wondered how it was he had got this opportunity instead of other people. In addition to this thinking, he talked about that although many eminent people in his field had told him that he was outstanding in his work, he could never accept that these evaluations were fully honest, or true. Ultimately, he had so little self-belief, that time and again, he talked himself out of following through on the ideas that we had agreed in our sessions. This frustrating and anxiety

> *inducing experience led him further into feelings of doubt, low self-belief, and even moments of despair.*
>
> *In the end, this highly skilled and professional person continued to do a good job, but at the cost of his overall well-being and personal flourishing, and experienced feelings of anger at not being able to use his skills and talents more fully.*

A final word

It is important to recognise that concepts like self-belief, the self, belief, and humility, are not static entities. In other words, there is a dynamic aspect in play here, which means that these qualities can be developed and grow, or be forgotten about and diminish.

In a high level performance environment, because these places constantly exert pressures to achieve and succeed on people, it is common to find that self-belief is frequently undermined. In some ways, this is a healthy situation psychologically speaking, since the person is reminded that they must always work on their self-belief as they would with anything else. It is also worth remembering that healthy self-belief is always accompanied by a small, yet significant, measure of self-doubt. It is essential that even those with the strongest self-belief remain aware that ultimately, their skills, abilities, and talents will fail, that is, prove insufficient to meet the challenge ahead, or task in hand.

It can often feel as though our self-belief is fragile, and that if we devote more effort to its development, we will *always* get the results we desire. Unfortunately, or maybe fortunately, human persons are not constituted in this fashion. Building strong self-belief is not a purely rational, systematic, and logical process. A key part of this task revolves around our subjective perceptions. In simple terms, self-belief is as much about our interpretation of things, as it is about the things themselves. For example, in my work I came across individuals who took time to reflect thoroughly and deeply on the reasons they should believe in themselves more than they did, and yet this did not always translate into improvements in self-belief. It seemed as though they still could not accept fully the talents they possessed, or achievements they had attained, because they were incapable of perceiving these qualities as belonging to them. During sessions, I would notice how anxious and even agitated people would become when they could see that self-belief depended as much on their perceptions, as reality. Dialogue during these moments sometimes had a circular quality, where the person would articulate the reasons for greater belief in themselves, and yet, find themselves ultimately unable to accept and embrace these reasons. Sometimes this condition appeared to be related to earlier moments in someone's life where important others had constantly undermined their self-belief; with other clients, it appeared to be closely related to a fear of responsibility. This idea connects to certain strands of existential phenomenological psychology, which highlight fear of responsibility as an unhealthy psychological condition.

The problem with responsibility, by which I mean being able to accept that you have free will to deny, or assent to something, is that it confronts someone with the real situation they find themselves in. Knowing that you have the skills and abilities to perform something, and believing that these are truly part of you, brings responsibility to use these wisely and fully. It seemed to me, that some people were afraid to take on this level of responsibility for their self-belief, because there would be no hiding place. This may sound like a very strange contradiction, a paradox even, that people will be prepared to identify solid reasons for self-belief, whilst at the same time try to ignore, or forget about these reasons. As a psychologist this can be a very frustrating experience, but it serves as an important reminder; all authentic learning can ultimately only take place, when the person is ready to step across the divide, that is, to fully take personal responsibility for the final stage in the learning process.

Arrogance or self-belief

As has been discussed in this chapter, very high levels of self-belief can, from an external perspective, appear to be a form of arrogance. One of the ways of differentiating between arrogance and deep self-belief is in relation to values. Arrogance is always self-sufficient and centred on only one thing; in what way will something benefit the individual themselves. The genuinely arrogant individual is just that an individual who distains other people, and is completely focused on their own self.

In contrast to this, I came across many sports persons who possessed, what I referred to as, healthy arrogance. To others, their level of self-belief seemed so incredible, that it was tempting to describe such people as arrogant. However, in dialogue with them, and also through the actions and attitudes they expressed in both small and large matters in their personal and professional lives, there were ample indicators that this perceived arrogance was of a different nature. The healthy aspect could be seen in these people in the way they were always open to the possibility of learning, even if somewhat paradoxically, they could appear more careful than most in being open to taking on new, or different ideas. My interpretation of this was that they often possessed considerable self-knowledge, and had personally engaged in what they had previously learned, and as a consequence, had great belief in this acquired material. However, they were usually the performers who asked the most questions and sought out new ideas, and this suggested to me that their (perceived) arrogance was tempered by moments of genuine humility.

As a last word on this state of affairs, I would say that the truly arrogant differ from those with a healthy arrogance because of a lack of genuine self-belief. Arrogant people are closed in on themselves, because ultimately they are insecure and afraid; they fear anything that will remind them that their knowledge is always incomplete, and that their abilities and skills will ultimately prove inadequate. Those who have attained high levels of genuine self-belief are invariably prepared to listen to new ideas, and welcome when their beliefs are challenged. They usually actively seek situations where they will have to confront uncomfortable questions about their strengths and weaknesses, including who they are, and what they stand for. This of course does not mean they accept these new ideas, or are prepared to change beliefs and practice quickly, or easily, since, as we have already said, they will have played a vigorous and active role in building their own self-belief. What it does mean however, is that they are always hungry to learn more, to test their beliefs to see if these can be improved upon. Whether their beliefs change as a result of this exposure to new ideas, or challenges, is often less important than the process, which helps the person to grow in self-knowledge and critical thinking.

4 Passion

I think the best place to start this chapter is to make it clear from the outset, that passion is most definitely not to be confused with the concept of motivation. One of the clearest ways to express this is from the words of two great teachers. The Scottish American founder of modern dance, Martha Graham, once observed that, *great dancers are not great because of their technique; they are great because of their passion.* Bill Shankly, the charismatic and highly successful manager of Liverpool football club in the 1960's and 70's, captured the importance of passion when he said that, *some people believe football is a matter of life and death. I am very disappointed with that attitude. I can assure you it is much more important than that.* I am sure Martha Graham and Bill Shankly would agree that motivation, especially intrinsic motivation, is important, but ultimately, it is passion which separates the very best from the merely good. As we will look at when discussing the concept of flow, motivation in psychology is most usually divided into intrinsic and extrinsic motives. Intrinsic motivation is often understood as a form of self-motivation. In other words, it is an explanation of why we do things for personal rewards. In contrast, extrinsic motivation refers to thoughts and behaviour driven by the hope of external rewards, such as, money, status, or winning.

Passion is more usually understood as being closely connected to emotion. In everyday language, it is common to hear the idea that being passionate is somehow to be over emotional. Very unfortunately, this quite limited and partial view of what constitutes passion and its importance in our lives has tended to be the starting place on the rare occasions that this concept has been considered in sports psychology. And although there are examples in the parent discipline of psychology of where passion has been treated more sympathetically, the dominant view appears to be that passion is a problem, and something which most definitely should not be encouraged.

If we leave the academic informed view for a moment, it is quite remarkable how passion is viewed so differently in the broader world. This very different perspective is arguably even more pronounced when we look at the field of sport. I would go as far to say that not only is passion viewed positively in professional sport, but that it is seen as one of the key psychological qualities that differentiates the best performers from others. Throughout my applied work in individual and team based sports, I would deliberately ask coaches and managers to list what they considered to be the most important psychological qualities they expected in their athletes. Although decision making, that is the ability to consistently make good choices under pressure, was frequently cited as the most important, passion was nearly always mentioned within the top four or five qualities. I have to say that when I probed further, I was told that whilst everyone in professional sport had ample levels of extrinsic motivation, the very best had retained high levels of intrinsic motivation, and crucially, seemed driven by a deeper passion for what they were doing. Depending on their interest in psychological matters, I would sometimes be able to interrogate these responses more fully, in order to understand why they felt that passion was mostly such a positive and essential psychological quality to possess.

I make no apologies that a considerable part of this chapter is based on my dialogue with these coaches, leaders, and managers about the concept of passion, as well as my observations of the athletes, especially at training and in competition. In this way, the content differs somewhat from other chapters of this book, in that less of this material is based on individual sessions with the athletes themselves.

Before turning attention to a more in-depth analysis of passion in sport, and how this can be used constructively and developed in everyone, I would like to return to the link between passion and emotion. Most approaches in psychology use the term emotion to refer to a wide range of feelings and states of arousal. For example, the study of emotion in the academic discipline of psychology could include looking at anger, fear, anxiety, and excitement. The dominant cognitive tradition in psychology gives the impression, at least, that emotion is something that happens to us, that it is a psychological condition which is not fully under our control, and may even be seen as dysfunctional and problematic. Emotion is often described within cognitive and similar approaches, as being something that interferes with focus, attention, decision making, and composure. A huge body of experimental and field based research confirms much of what we already know from our own lived experience.

Another view on this exists however, although it seems to have been forgotten or ignored to a large extent. It is empirically true that emotion, experienced in all its many different forms, has the potential to impair our thinking and behaviour. What seems to have been overlooked is that emotion can, in certain circumstances, be a helpful and positive feature. I believe that a realignment is necessary, and that data from the real world, the lived world of sport, needs to be included in our understanding and definition of passion in sport. To reduce passion to such simplistic notions as it being simply another name for being over-emotional is I believe, inaccurate, and also very poor science. Despite this, it seems that being passionate has been used negatively as shorthand for being out of control and irrational. In fact, although it is harder to find explicit reference to this idea in the sport literature, expressing oneself passionately is seen as immature and infantile behaviour, the sort of thing you would expect from inexperienced novices, and most certainly not from world class sports performers.

In this chapter, I hope to offer a more balanced perspective on the concept of passion, and one that those providing psychology support to athletes attend more closely to enable them to understand how this concept can be beneficial in the lives of those they are working with. In time, this may contribute to a shift in the academic literature, where passion is rehabilitated, and can be seen as something that has the potential to be very positive in all human lives, including those performing in highly stressful and challenging situations.

Sporting passions

If we look at how passion is dealt with by the sports media, it becomes clear that they tend to take a more positive view than is usually found in academic sport psychology literature. Reports are full of descriptions of athletes signing national anthems with passion, and how the passionate support from the fans helped the team fight back despite the odds. Journalists are not alone in this. Post-match interviews with coaches, managers, and the athletes themselves, frequently mention that victory was assured because the team or individual played with intense passion throughout the event, and most especially during setbacks. Again, it is very usual to listen to descriptions where passion and desire are mentioned in concert; they are often talked about as though they share a common root, which of course they do. The shared element it seems to me, is that both of these words convey the idea that something is taking place that is beyond mere motivation, or effort.

In an effort to get to the bottom of this relationship, and its meaning, I reflected on what I witnessed so often throughout my applied work. Although it might sound strange to more dry scientific minds, it seemed to me that desire and passion were expressions of a particularly intense form of love. I make no apologies for mentioning this powerful, misused, and to some ways of thinking, very unscientific word, at least in relation to professional sport. I often thought that there were many times during my professional life in sport and psychology, that I was watching a human activity infused with love. Not necessarily the type of love known as *caritas*, that is care and compassion for others, but definitely the love that allows a person to unreservedly commit their whole selves to something, or someone. And what's more, to do this not for immediate external reward, but to experience a type of self-fulfilment.

Later on in my career, I read something on love from Aristotle and Aquinas contained in the works of Josef Pieper, and immediately the links to passion were revealed. Passion is from the Latin term, *passio*, which can be translated as, suffering in order to achieve something we love. And with this definition from note, philosophers, and not as we might have expected, psychologists, I finally had some serious intellectual support for my conviction that passion, and being passionate in sport, might at least be not all bad. Indeed, given its connection to love, one of the most powerful words in human life, I began to appreciate why passion was feared, as much as it was welcomed. Something so strong might bring about great and good things, or plausibly, it could lead us in the opposite direction and cause much harm and worse.

I think at this point, I need to address a misunderstanding that is fairly common it seems to me, the confusion that arises when people talk about love as being passion. My reading and what I have seen lead me to think that passion is often part of love, but that love is a much broader and more complex concept than passion. This does nothing to diminish the importance of passion in sport, but does suggest that there is such a thing as positive helpful passion, as opposed to destructive and evil passion.

Passion as suffering

If we return for a moment to consider the etymological roots of the word passion, a very interesting idea becomes visible. Passion, as we have noted, can be defined as love accompanied by suffering. An important element in the description of passion is that it includes the notion of suffering willingly, that is, to accept and even embrace the reality of suffering.

I did see people in sport experience suffering, whether it was due to career ending injury, losing contracts, being vilified by the media unfairly, or failing at events they have dedicated their lives to winning. I have written about suffering and sacrifice previously in my earlier work (Nesti, 2007b), and contend they have the potential to be an important and positive feature in sport. In academic circles, the view has tended to be that sport is not the place to talk about such profound matters as sacrifice, and that real suffering cannot exist in this form of human activity. I have argued against these views, and feel they are based on an erroneous idea. I believe this view has been summed up nicely in the words of Schall (2012), that just because sport is based on play and therefore unserious, it is also deeply serious, as it is something we do for its own sake. In such a way, the professional sports person can be seen in similar ways to the musician, actor, or artist, and no one would be surprised to hear that their vocations can at times involve pain, sacrifices, or suffering.

Passion can be expressed in a number of different ways. I believe it is a serious misunderstanding to assume that passionate expression must also be highly emotional, and involve exuberant behaviour. In sport, especially at the highest levels, we often speak about performers possessing a slow burning passion, one that is in no way inferior to a more intense, visible, and short term experience.

In my work, I heard athletes, coaches, and other staff, talk about the deep passion they possessed for the sport they were involved with. It was clear to me from how they described this, and the different ways they expressed it in their daily lives, that this concept was very different to motivation. One of the ways I detected this was during moments of difficulty and challenge. In our one to one sessions, athletes would sometimes talk about their best performances as being those where they felt deeply passionate about what they were trying to do. Often in some detail, they would describe how they were able to go to extra levels, as they expressed it, where nothing was held back. A closer examination of this phrase revealed that on these occasions there was little fear of injury or failure, and that their overall sense was of being overtaken by some kind of pure love for what they were doing. When I listened carefully to their accounts, it was obvious that by love, they did not mean something gentle, weak, or disinterested. The type of love they were describing sounded a long way from romantic notions of deep joy and peace. No, the love they talked about ran alongside much discomfort, great effort, and even suffering, and felt as though, in their own words, everything they had, or were, was *being placed fully on the line*. This final phrase, extracted from dialogue with sports performers, suggests that passion involves the total dedication of our whole being for a task. Being here refers to the holistic concept of a person, that is mind, body, and spirit in a unified form.

Immediately, a new idea has become visible. To be passionate in behaviour or thought, involves a total giving without reservation. This pure level of intensity is something mentioned frequently when we describe the best in professional sport. In more ordinary language, we are talking about the capacity to engage whole heartedly, to avoid the temptation to hold anything back just in case things do not turn out as hoped for. I am convinced that it is this special psychological and spiritual quality of passion, which makes it one of the most sought after, and admired qualities of high level performance.

Helpful passion

I think there has been great confusion by assuming that because passion is associated with lack of control, coaches, and leaders try not to develop this in others. Whilst passion can lead to negative and destructive thoughts and behaviour, it clearly has the potential to galvanise the greatest and most outstanding of performances in professional sport.

Given the importance of passion in sport, there is a role for the coach, leaders, and psychologists especially, in helping to cultivate and harness this remarkable human quality. Although passion cannot be given to another person, and that to be genuine passion it must emerge from the individual person themselves, leaders and others, can create conditions where it can grow, and be used positively. One of the ways to achieve this is by example.

Leaders and coaches can demonstrate the value of passion through their own roles and activity. The careful use of words, as well as how they behave when confronting particular situations, can be a very powerful way to show how passion can be employed to good effect. I remember seeing one coach in professional cricket try to make sure that their passion for the game and competitive play did not hinder players, by making them over aroused or anxious. One of the ways they did this, was, to ask other staff or the psychologist, to observe and assess their coaching practice, and pay particular attention to what they said, and how they said it. This can be quite a challenge for anyone, but possibly more so for a person who is very good at what they do, and who has had great success formerly as a passionate player, or leader.

I remember thinking that it was somewhat paradoxical that the most passionate people, athletes, coaches, and other leaders, were often the most humble in terms of being prepared to seek out feedback on their practice, no matter how uncomfortable this might be. Once again, it reminded me that passion was not, as it often has been seen by psychology and sport psychology, some kind of irrational, or childish emotional outburst. True passion could more accurately be described as a psychological quality belonging to the very best, that is, those who, irrespective of physical and technical talents, give themselves over fully, without reservation, to the task in hand. And crucially, they do this out of love, as though something larger than themselves is guiding them to be this way.

When I had the opportunity to have dialogue with some of these impressive people and ask more about the passion they brought to the roles and tasks they carried out, I frequently came across two very important, and maybe to some, surprising factors. First, it became apparent that these passionate persons could not understand why anyone would be involved in their sport, at any level, if they were not in their words, "consumed by a healthy passion for what they were doing". I would ask if they had encountered others who did not have the passion for the sport they spoke about, and yet still performed well and achieved much. They usually acknowledged that such people could be found, but that there were few of these types of individuals at the very top of professional sport, and where they did exist, they felt these people had lost their passion along the way. In other words, such athletes and leaders started off with great passion for their chosen activities, and this had, alongside physical and technical talents, propelled them to such elevated levels. That they could still deliver at such levels now owed more to their exceptional talents, but the feeling was, that this could not be sustained in the longer term. In relation to this point, I believe one of the ways to define the very best is in relation to longevity in their desired vocation. This suggests that those whom retain passion for what they are doing throughout their careers, will be involved at the highest level of achievement over a considerable period of time. Inevitably, this will mean that they are very likely to achieve more than those who lose passion, and see it wane, or even disappear when they reach their goals. And what we know about the best in any performance domain, is that when they hit their goals, a re-setting takes place, and new goals are created.

The second point that was forcefully expressed to me on occasions, was that people with passion were usually much better team players, in that by caring so much about what they were doing, they would do as much as possible to support teammates to achieve their common goal. This passion could also be seen in a very striking way, for example, when a player, or coach, sacrificed their own needs or desires on behalf of the broader group. I was fortunate to work with people whose passion for the sport was such, that they would often place themselves in exceptionally difficult situations in order to help the team. For example, the best coaches I saw would protect players in public by ensuring that they accepted the responsibility for a poor performance or result, even though the reasons behind this unfortunate outcome were usually much more nuanced. This behaviour from head coaches, leaders, captains, and senior players often happened as a way of helping younger, or more inexperienced players.

This expression of passion has very little to do with being overly emotional or unstable, as seems to be the general view of passion in much of academic sport psychology. I would say that this type of sacrificial passion is actually the preserve of the most courageous, stable, and principled performers. This also introduces the idea that passion is grounded in ideas about morality and ethics. Or to express this another way, passion can be used to drive good outcomes, or bad. It might be that such a view could help some psychologists see this concept more favourably, and closer to how it is viewed by those who actually play, lead, and perform in the lived world of sport.

Something I often heard from both athletes and staff I worked with was, sometimes it felt that they no longer had the passion they possessed formerly. I distinctly remember one highly experienced professional international athlete, asking me if it was still possible to perform at the highest of levels when their passion for the game had all but gone. During our dialogue we looked at those inevitable moments, caused by prolonged absence from the team, injury, or ugly contractual difficulties, or where external events had contributed to diminished passion for playing and training. The athlete outlined in great detail that during these very unenjoyable periods of their career, they had found a way to maintain high standards, in part by reminding themselves that better times would eventually appear. They also talked about how they took great heart from remembering that this was their vocation, and something that was a huge part of their identity. Although very few individuals used the word vocation, it was clear to me that when they talked about fulfilling themselves, and doing what they were called to do, I knew that they were describing their involvement as being a vocation, as well as a career and a job. Within the session we looked closely at how this player had managed to rekindle their passion, and consider if this could be done in their current situation. On this particular occasion, the athlete could not see any way to reignite their deep passion for the sport, and now faced the question squarely, of whether it was possible to still perform at exceptional levels in the absence of passion.

The outcome from our work together was that this person began to develop a different relationship with their sport, one much more focused on how they could help their team mates become better, and what they wanted to achieve in the near future when they planned to leave the sport altogether. In other words, they knew that to perform at consistently elevated levels over a prolonged period length of time, could not be achieved without a burning passion for what they were doing. My interpretation of this, which was something I came across repeatedly, was that good performances and achievements were possible in the absence of passion, but the absence of passion would mean that there would be a time limit to how long this could be sustained. Interestingly, and given this book has emphasised that athletes are first and foremost human persons, I noticed that athletes and staff would talk about their passion being redirected into other areas of their life. On one such occasion, a very successful and outstanding Premiership footballer told me that their family and local community back in their home country was more the focus of their passion, compared to the sport. This passionate interest in something else did not appear to negatively affect their sport performance.

From the holistic perspective in psychology this is what we should expect, and in fact, I had many notes on sessions where athletes highlighted that passion for issues beyond their sporting lives helped them to enjoy an even longer career in sport. There were others, both athletes and staff, who felt that once their passion for sport had shifted elsewhere, it was time to move on and start a new phase of their life. Trying to explain to outside parties why someone at the peak of their powers might do such a thing, to leave early or retire prematurely, was an impossible situation to easily explain. I was fortunate however to come across some of these remarkable and courageous people, who decided to follow their passion to another place, and in so doing, begin to create a new identity for themselves.

A last word on the redirecting of passion to other interests. Broader, more personalist, and in-depth approaches, like existential and phenomenological psychology, do not see passion as a human quality that can ever be extinguished completely. Their view would be that passion is always present, although its strength and focus might differ at different times. The practical question emanating from this psychological account, is therefore, about how we help people to continue to find areas in their life, personal or professional, where the continuous stream of passion can be directed.

In my work with professional sport, I rarely came across anyone who had not experienced a deep passion in relation to what they were doing, what they could achieve, or what they hoped for. In contrast to this, accounts from clinical psychology with people suffering from various forms of mental ill health, indicates that many of these persons have lost the feeling of passion in their lives. It seems as though the concept of passion also implies that someone has to be able to leave their own narrow interests and immediate concerns behind, and as a result can really only take place when a person unreservedly throws themselves into some kind of act. And to be able to leave the self behind, to diminish our ego, and engage in such a pure and fulsome way, cannot be done by the person who is suffering from neurotic anxiety, or clinical depression. It seems from this we might tentatively be able to say, that passion, and being able to be passionate are good indicators of psychological health and human flourishing.

More passion

In relation to this broader conceptualisation of passion it might be important to recognise that this is not a skill as such, although it can, like a skill or technique, aid performance and achievement. A question arising from this is: if passion is not a discrete skill, how can we learn and develop this? I would argue that as a holistic psychological quality, people are already endowed with passion as part of being human. I realise that this argument is one about ontology, that is, what is it that makes us human. Or to put this another way, what are the universal givens of human life, encountered and experienced by all, throughout cultures and over time, if passion is already there so to speak? The question therefore, is how can awareness of this fact be used to enhance human flourishing and achievement in sport and elsewhere.

It is worth noting that Aquinas distinguished between the value of two ways of being passionate. His helpful insight was to point out that to propose something, or act *out* of passion, is quite different to doing something *with* passion. In his very measured and precise way, he has introduced two crucial features by this description. To do something out of passion is to be avoided, since this is when pure emotion and subjectivity take the lead, and poor, unethical, or morally bad decisions might be made. In contrast, acting with passion, is seen as something wholesome, and which has the potential to assist human happiness and performance. Now when I first came across this, I smiled to myself thinking how many athletes and coaches, especially those who had left school with few, if any academic qualifications, sounded like Thomist philosophers! But then, since his philosophy has been described, and sometimes condescendingly derided, as being philosophical realism, and mere common sense, I shouldn't have been surprised that real people, in the real life of sport, would see things this way. It made me reflect once again, that academic sport psychology, in dismissing the value of passion, was at least half right according to this description provided by Aquinas. Unfortunately, they seem to have missed that although acting *out* of passion is a problem, acting *with* passion is often found in the very best.

One of the interesting features about passion expressed in practice is the idea of controlled passion. At first glance, the phrase controlled passion, sounds like a contradiction. If passion involves a kind of spontaneous and intense emotional response, it is difficult to see how this fits easily with notions of control and direction. I witnessed many examples of controlled passion in the lives of the professional sports performers and leaders I was fortunate enough to observe at close quarters. They seemed to understand that passion was not equivalent to being excessively emotional, or beyond control, and that it was possible to harness passionate thoughts and feelings to assist performance, especially where this involved considerable endurance.

In watching and listening to athletes with passion, I saw, that like most other psychological aspects of human persons, this quality could fluctuate. On occasion, the visible expression of passion was easy to see and detect, and at other times it was more hidden from view. Nevertheless, in dialogue with many athletes and staff, I was told that even when passion was difficult to see externally, within the individual they were aware of a burning desire to empty themselves for the task in hand. And what's more, to do this on their own terms, willingly, and out of love for what they were doing. These phenomenological descriptions from the lived world of professional sports people, made it clear to me that passion was not to be confused with motivation, and neither was it to be reduced to a temporary emotional outburst. Their descriptions of passion also helped to clarify that both a feeling of sacrifice and love were at the core of this special human psychological quality.

A surprising support for the conviction that sport can involve moments of passion, sacrifice, and love can be found, albeit indirectly, in the magnificent work of the German philosopher, Joseph Pieper. In his book, *Leisure the basis of culture*, he describes how human activity beyond the world of work, gives meaning to life and explains why the ancient Greeks claimed that *we work so we can have leisure*. In a reversal of the hierarchy of values that has largely dominated Western thinking since the Reformation and Renaissance, Pieper contends that leisure, broadly conceived, is at once the most useless and indispensable feature of human life. In this paradoxical statement he is expressing the counter cultural idea that although work is very important and provides useful outcomes, it is during our acts of leisure that we become fully human.

By leisure, he is referring to all areas that do not fall under the term work. And although he tends to write mostly about the arts, music, poetry, painting, and sculpture, he makes it clear that any human activity beyond work, can serve this vital purpose in our lives. It is quite obvious that no one would deny the sacrifices involved in becoming a great artist in any medium, and yet, the dominant view at least in psychology, sport psychology, and even sports philosophy, is that since sport is really just another form of play, such a dense theological and philosophical term like sacrifice is inapplicable.

When I listened to athletes who were battling through recovery periods from serious injury or illness, they frequently told me that they could only continue to make the necessary sacrifices because their passion for the sport remained undiminished. Sometimes they would talk about how they felt very anxious about the progress of their rehabilitation work, and also that their motivation was at an all-time low. When asked about how they kept doing the necessary work to allow them to return to the action, I was told many times that even though they hated not being able to train or play, their passion helped them to keep moving forward when the easier thing might be to give up. And not infrequently, with athletes facing these existentially difficult moments, something I have referred to before as *critical moments*, the voice would waver and tears would flow.

Of course, there are many ways to interpret these reactions when facing critical moments, and I believe one of the most important is to see this in terms of the possible obliteration of a particular identity, and the anxiety associated with moving into the unknown. In addition to this, I am sure that what was taking place in those encounters was a very vivid and visceral expression of a deep passion. Although maybe not at those moments but rather during later reading and reflection, I would return to the definition of Aquinas that passion refers to suffering for a love. And this suffering, this sacrifice for something not yet attained, was done willingly, voluntarily by the person themselves.

In my one to one encounters, I began to see that the existence of passion was essential when facing moments of extreme adversity. In the everyday language of some of the best coaches I came across, passion to do the right things, and do them for longer than anyone else, was most important when the team or person were "up against it!" Passion, as a way of helping the person to face up to and overcome adversity, is something well understood in the best cultures and environments. It is as though leaders in these situations understood that to overcome great challenges, something extra is often required. This, once again, may sound like a contradiction, given that this chapter is based on a psychological perspective which argues that all human beings are endowed with passion as something innate. One of the questions that flows from this, is how do we encourage passion for the best of things, those that aid human flourishing and performance.

Beyond this though is the idea that great passion will be required to take on huge challenges. If the level of human passion has been stunted or undermined in people, either through external conditions, the culture, or by their own choices, it becomes difficult to find passionate people. In my experience, many of the people I worked with had retained a deep passion for their sport and saw this as an opportunity to fulfil themselves, to literally pursue this activity to become the best version of themselves possible. That this desire for authenticity and self-expression was also accompanied by the natural desire for extrinsic rewards, like wealth, fame, and accolades, is only to be expected. As we have discussed earlier, intrinsic and extrinsic motivation are both important and healthy, and feature in most areas of life.

Finally, when facing the difficult moments of frequent defeats, underperformance, and other types of failure, I saw and heard leaders remind players that they needed to start again, and bring everything they had to the match or competition, and in their words, "to leave it all out there". Occasionally, the word passion, might be expressed at these moments. In my view, whether the word was said or not didn't really matter, as it was quite clear that individuals' were being asked to go out and suffer, and to sacrifice everything they had on behalf of something they loved. The very best I was so lucky to spend time with, called on their reserves of passion time and time again, to allow them, no matter how arduous the circumstances, *to act with passion but not out of passion*.

5 Flow play and happiness

If I had to choose one psychological concept that has been the best received amongst high level professional sports people, it would have to be Mihalyi Csikszentmihalyi's idea of flow. When asking athletes to describe the psychological conditions surrounding their very best performances, most begin to list in some detail the key elements of flow. Described by Jackson and Csikszentmihalyi (1999) in terms of nine discrete factors, I was always excited and reassured to hear such shared experiences, often across a wide range of sports, each demanding very different physical and technical abilities, and skills. In my work I would often listen to athletes talking about how flow impacted them beyond their immediate performance. This is remarkably close to the notion put forward by sport psychologist and Catholic priest, Pat Kelly, who carried out PhD studies with Csikszentmihalyi. Kelly observed, *although a person doesn't have attention to explicitly think of himself during flow, afterward when he does have such attention available, he is aware that his self has grown.*

Athletes and support staff would talk about feeling at one with the task in hand, being totally focused on one thing at a time, and this experience invariably feeling without obvious effort, or strain. It is well known that in some sports, flow is described as "being in the zone", or alternately, having a mentality of being "in the moment". Although there are considerable similarities between these terms, I have always found that Csikszentmihalyi's original work on flow provides the most complete and useful account of this phenomenon. A close reading of the flow literature since Csikszentmihalyi's initial studies some 50 years ago, and especially after his first book in 1975 on this topic, suggests that the flow state is not only where we perform our best, but is where we are happiest. In relation to enjoyment and happiness, American professor of political science, James Schall, has even linked flow to the concept of love. Schall proposed that, a *good game again takes us out of ourselves, but it is only when we are most "out of ourselves" that we are most ourselves. Not only do we speak of our minds taking us out of ourselves, but we find that our loves do the same thing.*

Csikszentmihalyi's initial studies into flow were guided by phenomenology. This is a very important feature because phenomenological psychology aims to describe an experience in the words of the person who experiences the event. A term which has become well used, but apparently less well understood, is that of the *Lebenswelt*, or lived world. This concept is one of the most important in phenomenology and phenomenological psychology; it describes how we experience and encounter the world, prior to reflection, analysis, or evaluation. For a more comprehensive introduction to this complex idea, I have suggested a number of introductory books and articles in the bibliography which may be of interest. For the purpose of this chapter, I will restrict myself to noting how phenomenology could be used to allow practitioners of any sort, or researchers, to understand psychological phenomena more closely to the way they are encountered, and experienced by people themselves. I believe that the vast body of research into the flow state, demonstrates the unique value of using the phenomenological method in psychological studies.

The actual term, flow, emerged from some of Csikszentmihalyi's earliest research with heart surgeons, artists, professional athletes, and other performers. Flow represents a phenomenological term, rather than an abstract or theoretical construct, because it was the word spontaneously chosen by a range of high performing individuals to describe how they felt, and thought, during their own best performances. This word then, flow, is very much in keeping with the rest of the psychological terms and concepts discussed within this book. As was explained in the introduction, the chapters and headings of this book represent what I experienced as the most important psychological ideas mentioned by my clients, rather than concepts or constructs directly from psychological, or sport psychology, literature.

Listening carefully to the wide range of people I have been able to work with over so many years, has reinforced my view that the flow experience is felt by everyone, and welcomed universally. Csikszentmihalyi, and the great number of studies that flowed from his initial research, found that the flow state can take place in almost any human activity, across people from different cultures, with differing traditions, and in a huge variety of roles. Through my reading around this concept since I first opened his book, *Beyond boredom and anxiety*, and guided by the testimonies of so many of the professional sports people I have known, led me to reflect on two very important aspects about flow. I intend to look more closely at these two interrelated ideas within this chapter, and offer suggestions on what we can do, personally and collectively, to allow flow to happen more frequently.

Sometimes during dialogue, I would hear a person complain that they could no longer get into a flow-like psychological state because they had begun to develop an excessively instrumental and utilitarian approach to a particular task, their work, or role. When we looked in greater depth at some of the possible reasons behind this frustrating situation, it often became apparent that there had been a very important change in their relationship to what they were doing. This worrying state of affairs was often explained in their own words as, "I have fallen out of love with what I am doing!" A closer examination of what lay behind this phrase would frequently reveal that for this individual, what they were engaged in, was now carried out purely to gain external rewards. In the language of cognitive psychology, the person was unable to experience the flow state because their focus was totally on extrinsic rewards, with the result that their intrinsic motivation had been lost.

Again, and it may sound very surprising given the high level that some of these athletes performed at on a daily basis, people would express frustration that they had lost all sense of playfulness and enjoyment in what they were doing, and that spontaneity, intuition, and even creativity, had become very hard to find.

Given how important enjoyment of the task is in achieving flow, I will spend time describing how I worked with individuals to help them to recover the necessary balance between extrinsic and intrinsic motivation, and re-discover a playful spirit, to allow more frequent and deeper experiences of flow. Although not always mentioned in the literature on Flow, I came to understand that the concept of play, and playing, was absolutely central to understanding flow, and its connection to psychological flourishing and performance. In looking briefly at play in this chapter, I would like to suggest that sport psychology, and indeed all branches of psychology, need to attend more closely to this universal human phenomenon, and begin to see it as essential to all people, not only children, or novices.

Flow cultures

Sometimes though, the lack of flow seemed to be more the result of factors largely beyond the control of the person themselves. Although this area of concern has not usually been given as much attention as personal factors in attaining flow, I believe it is an important part to appreciating why flow is harder to achieve in some situations than others. During person to person encounters in my work, I would frequently listen to people criticising coaching practices, work processes, organisational environments, and cultures. These were singled out as often getting in the way of creating the optimal conditions for flow to take place. Individuals described how particular sets of circumstances acted as obstacles, and made it harder for them to enter and remain in flow. For example, an environment where focus was exclusively on outcomes, whether this was results or material successes, was often associated with difficulties around flow. Coaches who over-emphasised external factors, or largely used coercion and punishments to achieve the desired behaviours, created climates that were anti-flow. In these oppressive, negative anxiety filled, and distressing environments, where scrutiny seemed all pervasive, and little joy was evident, individuals would typically find it very hard to adopt a more playful, process focussed mentality in their work. It was in these cultures and environments where I often found myself spending more time with coaches and other support staff to help influence their work practices and communication, to attempt to build a more flow friendly culture.

I have to say that the higher the level I worked at, the more receptive the staff were to this message. At first glance this might appear to be yet another paradox. At least from a rational perspective, it might be expected that when the stakes are highest, there would typically be little room, and even less need, to encourage the playful psychological state known as flow. I found that at the most elite levels, there was a deep appreciation of the need to create the best external conditions to allow for more flow. This understanding came less from extensive reading and study, and was more from the lived experience of the coaches especially. The best operators in this group remembered that as players and athletes themselves, many of their best performances had been accompanied by some level of flow experience. In addition to what they had encountered in their earlier playing careers, staff and coaches could also see that the most optimal and enjoyment filled moments in their roles as leaders, usually took place when they could do their work in an environment that was more conducive to flow. The challenge facing the staff as leaders in their respective roles, was about finding the courage to create a culture that did not crush the athlete's intrinsic motivation for what they were doing, whilst being able to maintain a necessary level of structure, organisation, and rules.

More flow

The most experienced and highest achieving persons I worked with could recount having many moments of flow throughout their careers. Using vivid language to convey how they thought and felt during these experiences, much of what was said was very close to what was reported in the scientific literature on flow. People talked about feeling at one with the task they were doing, lost in the moment, feeling calm and in control, but without any anxiety, strain or obvious effort. After the event they conveyed how tired and even exhausted they felt, and that they often had an unusual feeling of gratitude, or joy. This was sometimes coupled with the thought that this moment had just appeared by chance, and that what they did was not fully within their control. All in all, I heard these ideas expressed about everything from the smallest most private events, to tasks taking place in front of millions of people live, and on television. And not surprisingly, there was a keen interest in having these types of experiences more often, both in training and competitive events.

Before looking at how increases in flow could take place, I would like to mention what at first may sound like a contradiction. Throughout my applied practice and research, there seemed to be one category of person who had great difficulty attaining the flow state. Despite strong research findings supporting real-world practice that the best performers tended to have the most flow, and feel this state most deeply, this did not mean that there was always a clear correlation between the level of athlete, and the experience of flow. In my own early research carried out on postgraduate studies at the University of Alberta, I discovered that whilst some of the top ranked swimmers in Canada reported the highest levels of flow, a group just outside of the very best in the country rarely had any flow experiences at all. In contrast, the good level recreational and lower level club swimmers were second only to the highest ranked performers in terms of the frequency, and intensity, of reported flow states. The design of my study allowed me to assess levels of intrinsic motivation alongside measuring for flow. What I discovered, was the middle group of highly proficient, but not top national level swimmers, had very low levels of intrinsic motivation. Specifically, they reported that they did not feel especially competent, and had lost any sense that swimming competitively was something they had largely chosen to do. In cognitive psychological terminology these constructs are referred to as perceived competence, and feelings of self-determination.

Over the years in my applied practice, I noticed how often I would come across this finding from this study I did in Canada in 1988; time and again, I found that flow was strongest in the most elite performers, and the serious recreational competitive groups, but rarely evident in those just below the very best.

There are several possible explanations for this finding, but I would like to highlight two reasons I believe to be most likely. To get into the flow state requires, amongst other things, that attention is directed at the task in hand only, and not at the possible rewards, or negative repercussions which could follow upon completion of the task. In dialogue with those who had few flow experiences, I discovered that they had largely lost all interest in doing the sport for its own sake, for the joy in doing something they had chosen to do, and felt good at. Instead, their focus was only on what they could get by succeeding in the task. As a result, focus was on hoped for future outcomes, and not the execution of the task itself. The result was that with such a distracted focus, their performances were below what they might have expected given their level of skill and ability. Added to this, was the issue of anxiety. This was not the anxiety we will look at more fully in the final chapter of the book, the kind that is often accompanied by excitement, and can arise when we face a challenge we are well prepared for, and care about. No, this anxiety was only about thoughts of failure, losing, and not getting the result, or outcome hoped for. Anxiety, as we know from our own encounter with this normal human psychological state, is the result of projecting our mind into the future, and hoping that things will turn out well. The problem is that if our mind is on the future it is unable to attend sufficiently to the present, then the result will be poor task focus, and energy wasted on trying to control something we have no complete control over-the future outcome. Sometimes this can create a cycle, and push the person further into the distracted and uncomfortable feeling of this type of anxiety, and leads to where our thoughts are completely confused, and we feel as if we are disintegrating.

My work with this middle group of low flow people was often a failure, until they were prepared to re-orient their focus on finding enjoyment in what they were doing, and resist the temptation to look too far ahead at things largely outside their immediate control.

The moment where recognition and acceptance of the need to reduce focus on extrinsic rewards, and return to greater levels of intrinsic motivation, was very often at what existential psychology refers to as, *boundary situations*. Boundary situations are those occasions when we face a personally meaningful and significant challenge to our normal way of doing things. These are opportunities to reflect on what we usually do, and to find a new way, or return to earlier solutions. Never easy to face because the barrier is often our own selves, these can be times when the personal conditions to gain more flow can be established. With my professional sports clients, this frequently came during difficult times, such as facing the possibility of being sold to other clubs, being dropped from the starting side for months on end, failing to make cuts, injury problems, personal issues, or any other tough periods. Very often, the best way to deal with this, for the athlete, or member of staff, was to re-discover a sense of enjoyment in what they were doing. These difficult moments could additionally serve to help people reflect, more honestly and deeply, on why they were doing what they were doing.

Instead of relying on more superficial techniques like mental skills training, some clients would use these occasions to ask deeper questions about purpose and meaning. For example, this could involve a person re-evaluating what made them happy in what they were doing, and helped them develop a new relationship to their work.

In a way, this could be seen to be an example of where adversity, and a lack of flow, brought a person to a moment of crisis. Typically, they would be faced with trying to patch up their existing situation in order to get through, or accept the need to make a more profound and fundamental change. I sometimes felt honoured to listen to people during these difficult times, who would confirm that their career had become totally about extrinsic motives, and now only served a utilitarian purpose. This psychological condition brought little personal happiness and joy, and prevented them from achieving better performances.

An advantage of working with highly talented or experienced people during these boundary situations, was that they almost always had memories of times in their development and career in the sport, where intrinsic and extrinsic motivation were kept in balance. These moments usually occurred when their focus was on performing the task for itself, and as best as possible. During descriptions of these special phases of someone's life, it was not uncommon for persons to become very animated and emotional. I remember one striking example of this when a player visualised when, in their words, "they were happily lost in just playing the game". At this point in the encounter, they broke down in tears. When we looked back at this difficult session, the person could see that their reaction was a mixture of deep upset at how different many of their experiences had since become. There was also an awareness of how much they still loved what they did, and how important it was to their identity, despite so many unpleasant and challenging moments.

A bit more flow

Over the years, I began to realise that Ken Ravizza's (1977) wisdom in relation to the frequency of flow in elite sport, had very important consequences for my work. Although efforts were made to alter personal and external psychological conditions to increase the likelihood of flow, data from many of my highest achieving clients revealed that they were, somewhat paradoxically, the most personally comfortable when not in flow. This group seemed to have understood that the challenge to performance success would reside as much in what they did when not in flow, as when they were in that special optimal psychological state.

We began to describe this as, B minus, or C plus, *flow-like* psychological states. This described where the vast majority of performers often found themselves psychologically, and involved many of the factors associated with flow, but crucially, experienced with less intensity, and frequency. One of my athletes, who I was with for many years, referred to this as a *flow-light* condition, one that mostly was good enough to get the job done, but not much more than that. When looking at how this was experienced in practice, I heard that one of the advantages was that this less than optimal flow state could help performers transition into genuine flow. My understanding of this was that the boundary between these two states was not as large as it may have seemed, and during performances, the flow-light stage could sometimes provide a platform for the person to move across into more authentic true flow.

There was also a further very attractive aspect to this. Being in a flow-light place logically meant that the performer was not in somewhere much worse. The best understood the need to accept that they could perform well in this less than comfortable zone, which reduced the likelihood of them collapsing into a zone of catastrophic performance, and most likely complete failure. The understanding to accept that performance could still be at a good level, but maybe not the best, when in the flow-light zone, was something I felt was closely connected to Ken Ravizza's famous dictum: *the best are comfortable being uncomfortable*!

I frequently worked with people who would apparently sabotage their own performances if they were not feeling as though they were in flow. They seemed committed to the idea that if something did not feel easy, effortless, and anxiety free, for example, their subsequent performance levels would be incredibly low. One of them called this phenomenon, psychological greed. By this rather brutal term, she meant that someone wanted to have more than they were entitled to, or could ever be attained realistically. As they and several other performers acknowledged, and for which there exists strong support in the academic sports psychology literature, being permanently in a complete state of pure flow is not possible for any human being. To search for this impossible event is likely to cause more anxiety, demotivation, and even despair. To help persons facing these situations, dialogue would be about revealing how reasonably good work, and some level of enjoyment, could still be experienced during moments of less than optimal flow.

Vignette: finding flow by not looking for flow

I had worked for a number of years with a highly experienced and successful individual professional athlete who wanted to have more moments of flow in their performances. They would tell me in great detail about occasions where they were able to stay present focused, remain in the moment, and get into the flow state. Their descriptions sounded as though they were reading from the list of nine factors identified by Jackson & Csikszentmihalyi which often accompany being in flow. We would agree in our dialogue that the aim was to create conditions, internally and externally, to get more flow, whilst always accepting that even for the very best, the reality will be that most of the time we will be unable to achieve flow, and must still be able to produce strong work, even when not in this special psychological state. Unfortunately, accepting that the majority of what we do, even if we are world class performers, will not take place in flow, is a very bitter pill to swallow for anyone. It is may be even be harder for those who have experienced how this psychological state, which sounds so simple to achieve, has helped them deliver their very best ever performances during moments of greatest challenge. It might sound strange to say, but having seen the power of flow in their own lives, elite level professional athletes can become obsessed with getting more of this state. The main problem with this mentality is that the more we want flow and try to get it, the less we are likely to achieve it. My athlete would begin to talk about flow as though it was something they could work on in a structured and systematic way. And as we will see, although there are many things that can be done to make it more likely that flow will appear, it never appears if we go searching for it. We would talk about how flow did not just happen by chance, and yet, somewhat paradoxically, it could not be forced to happen. Eventually my client would describe the kind of things they could do to create the best conditions for flow. We would look at how important it was for them not to work with coaches who built excessive performance anxiety in them, undermined their self-belief, or prevented them having any input into their choices around training, tactics, and the like. They recognised that an excessive focus on the important but problematic sources of extrinsic motivation usually needed some level of adjustment. For example, they would refuse to do goal setting, and try to keep a season long focus as much as possible on performance and learning, in comparison to winning and achievements. From a more personal and internal psychological perspective, effort would be made to remind themselves repeatedly, and especially near events, that they had the skills and abilities needed to do well in the task. These specific psychological tactics and approaches were carried out with much care and attention. And yet, time and again, when the athlete took part in important competitions they would fail to experience as much flow as they hoped for, at least until they knew they were not going to achieve their competitive aims. Only at these moments, when all seemed lost, were they suddenly able to play with freedom, to stay in the moment, and get into deep flow states. But by now, in terms of gaining success in their competitive event or match, it was all over, and they were now playing just to finish the task. The frustration that this caused, and even despair, was psychologically very damaging to the athlete. They would try again and again, but the physical, psychological, emotional, and spiritual toll on the person, over years of this struggle, was very considerable.

When we looked back to see how this had taken place so many times in their career, we concluded that a major issue was that despite all of the excellent work to make room for more flow, the athlete always doubted their own ability, despite others telling them how good they really were. It seemed that coming to the sport through different channels and later than many of their contemporaries had left a wound, where deep down they never really perceived they had the competence to achieve at this level of competition. For some athletes, such an unorthodox path to the top might have worked the other way around psychologically, and told them that they had an incredible natural talent to be able to play at such high standards despite a very late start in the sport. It seemed that the athlete was fully aware of the power of flow and how it took

> place alongside their best performances and most enjoyable moments, and yet they could not manage to free themselves enough in event, in the heat of competition, to achieve this desired psychological state. Much of our work together was oriented to trying to accept that good or even very good performances were still possible when not in flow, albeit they might not feel good, or be especially comfortable. Unfortunately, the athlete was largely unable to accept the reality that good enough work could be done outside of flow, and their career as a result was quite short. In the end, it became just too psychologically exhausting as well as financially difficult, to experience only a very small number of exceptional performances in flow, in contrast to the anxiety filled, frustrating and despair inducing poor performances which made up the majority of their professional life.

Flow and play

If we look more carefully at the description of flow provided by Csikszentmihalyi, it is clear to see that it closely resembles psychological accounts of play. Catholic priest, university academic, and sport psychologist, Pat Kelly, who carried out PhD work under Mihalyi Csikzentmihalyi, has written extensively about the link between play and flow, and is someone who has argued that sport, and sport psychology by extension, needs to take the concept of play more seriously.

His account of why play is not considered as a topic for serious study, or research in sport-related studies, draws on a number of very interesting perspectives. Kelly (2023) explains that play has typically been viewed as being about fun, something not normally associated with serious sport, and usually a word we think of when we discuss children's sport. He suggests that this myopic view is partly because of theological and philosophical changes that took place in Western countries as a result of the Reformation, when some strands of Protestant thinking over emphasised the importance of work, and denigrated the notion of play. And as an American academic drawing on his deep knowledge of sport at all levels in the United States, Kelly notes that the problem of play has been especially acute throughout the history of sport in his country. The dominance of the protestant work ethic in the broader culture has to a large extent been mirrored in North American sport, especially at collegiate and professional levels. Very often, the notion that sport can involve play, creativity, inventiveness, spontaneity, and even beauty, is viewed with suspicion, or outright hostility. At times it can even sound as though play and being playful is considered to be unethical, not fair even, and close to cheating. For a fuller account of this negative view of play in Anglo Saxon cultures particularly, I would recommend a short book by Josef Pieper called, *Leisure: the basis of culture* (1963). Pieper's work addresses the psychological and spiritual damage done to human persons by basing our existence on an exclusively materialist philosophy that is grounded in a one-sided rationalist outlook, and which has variously led to reductionism, scientism, and the denial of human free will. It seems that this eminent philosopher is convinced that the concept of leisure, including play, is a very

Flow play and happiness 73

serious and important matter, and has implications for our psychological flourishing, experience of flow, happiness, and spiritual health.

In my applied work with professional athletes and support staff, I would often come across the term play. Performers would talk about how they had lost their enjoyment of what they were doing, and that actions felt overly mechanical, constrained, and predictable. Depending on the sport, role, or position, this lack of playfulness could cause great difficulties, and prevent the athlete from achieving their desired outcomes. Given the well-established link between playfulness, creativity, and spontaneity, the lack of this quality in some cases resulted in players losing their place in the team, and even managers and their staff being sacked.

I often saw situations where an excessive focus on the necessary, but never sufficient quality, of hard work and effort, reduced the scope for creative playful action, and by extension, meant that individuals and the team were rarely operating in a flow state. The result of this, in part at least, was that performances declined and results were poor. It even got to the situation, where the media joined in the criticism, complaining that the team, and certain individuals, were merely a group of hard working athletes, and that as everyone knows, hard work alone is not enough to succeed at the very highest of levels.

Creativity, inventiveness, spontaneity, and imagination, all of which take place in flow states and play, are an essential part of optimum performance. In addition, there is research to support this idea from the thousands of published studies into flow, and peer-reviewed articles in psychology journals on play and learning, and playfulness, creativity, and performance.

Play and flow are not only directly associated with better performances, but of maybe even greater import, they are mentioned alongside happiness and enjoyment. I would often listen to those in professional sport talking about the need to get back to enjoying what they did; to feeling happy more frequently. Inevitably, these types of dialogue took place during challenging periods, particularly when performances and results were not going well. I am sure it will sound surprising to some, but during difficult times, athletes and staff were not necessarily looking to work harder. Often I would hear that if anything, teams and individuals were actually working *too hard*, and what was now needed was the courage, and I do mean that word, to adopt a more relaxed and carefree (not careless though) mentality. This would hopefully allow players a chance to play more deeply, which could increase moments of flow and enjoyment.

Play and the spirit of playfulness, which are so closely connected to the idea of flow states, are in my experience of huge importance in all sport. I believe they are as relevant to top level professionals, as to youth, and amateur sport. Although it is possible to interpret this statement in a number of ways, I am convinced that when serious high level professional performers talked to me about wanting to play more like they did when younger, or at earlier periods of their careers, they really meant the word play. I would ask them to tell me what this was like, and how it would feel and look. This approach is consistent with phenomenological psychology where the first act is to get the person to look carefully and closely at what they are talking about, and then to describe this in as much detail as possible.

During these moments, it was not uncommon for athletes to become quite animated and passionate as they spoke about occasions and situations where they allowed themselves to play, or played with greater freedom. Now, I believe that these two phrases, playing with freedom, and giving oneself permission to play, despite what we might initially think, are very deep and profound psychological ideas.

If we turn first to the idea that we sometimes feel as though we need to give ourselves permission to play, it seems to suggest that more play, and getting into a spirit of play, depends to some extent, on limitations we place on ourselves. I have always been so impressed to listen to highly experienced coaches and managers, most of whom had been former professional players themselves, encouraging individuals and teams to allow themselves to perform, through playing more intensely, and fully. They would sometimes express this in what at first sounded like a very strange thing to hear in top level professional sport. These leaders would ask the athletes to, *"go out there and play, have fun, and really enjoy yourselves!"*

In relation to these ideas about the desire to be more playful, I feel some researchers, coaches, and consultants in sport and performance psychology, have not paid sufficient attention to the lived world, and words used by those on the ground. It has often seemed to me that instead of taking the athletes seriously, many psychologists and coaches have come in with pre-conceived notions. An especially damaging idea, is the unempirical and rather arrogant assertion, that those operating in sport, or any other area of human endeavour at the very highest of levels, have no time for wasteful and frivolous concepts like play. I think those holding this perspective have missed the point hugely. It could be that this really reflects their own attitude in that they cannot see how play, or a playful spirit, can lead to excellence, and human happiness, because they themselves do not possess this quality in their lives, or work. I feel that such a view is a major problem, because it means these psychologists, coaches, or leaders, will be unable to understand what the greatest artists, scientists, educators, athletes, and others, already know; almost all great work in these respective fields arises through a combination of hard work, and by adopting a playful attitude. If this is doubted, then a brief reading about the lives of Mozart, Einstein, Federer, and Messi, will reveal this truth.

Permission to play

As a psychologist, I was always very impressed to listen to staff in Premiership football changing rooms, on training grounds, and before major sporting events, trying to instil a more play like, and playful spirit, in their athletes. In my work during confidential one to one sessions, the athletes' often mentioned how much they welcomed coaches' encouragement, but ultimately they knew that permission to set themselves free to play, and be more playful in their work, had to come from themselves.

In this dialogue, invariably athletes would return to specific moments where they adopted a more playful attitude in their work. Very often these would be during earlier stages of their career, or as children, and youth athletes. I did wonder if athletes might be tempted to dismiss these earlier experiences as not being relevant to the more elevated and highly pressured levels they now operated at, but typically they would reject this, and tell me that being courageous enough to play at earlier stages in their journey was as hard, if not even more difficult, than when they were more established and secure.

In this, I believe they made an excellent of often overlooked point, that the pressure to get on the ladder and make it to the next stage, meant that it was very easy to be tempted to adopt a more cautious, workmanlike, and controlled approach in their performances, to try to get the job done, and achieve selection. And yet, irrespective of personality type (NB: I always did a brief personality assessment of my clients in the first session, to help with our dialogue, and make the supplementary point that persons are so much more than just their personalities), almost all talked about being able to really show who they were, and what they could do, by playing as though nothing serious was at stake. This is not an easy thing to carry out, when the reality was that their life dream might be there on the line, and was related ultimately to how they would perform.

Athletes, and even leaders and coaches, would describe how to return to more playfulness, and a spirit of play, the challenge would be in their own words, to *lift off* the baggage they had accumulated, that now served to hide the real person. When we looked at this baggage it became clear this was often ideas, restrictions, and constraints, the person had put on themselves over time. It frequently consisted of doing things to please others, not wanting to stand out from the crowd, or avoiding the responsibility for failures. Athletes and staff also said this centred on hoping that just doing their jobs would be enough, since it is physically and psychologically exhausting always having to give everything, all the time. In more psychological terminology, I believe they were referring to the anxiety of freedom, avoiding the discomfort of being more authentic, and following a natural desire to achieve things more easily than before. Interestingly, the biggest catalyst for change was not only about enhancing performance, but was more often related to enjoyment. Athletes would talk about wanting to play again, so they could truly enjoy what they were doing. They recognised that this type of enjoyment was not only a key to better performances, but crucially, the best way to remain at the highest level for as long as possible.

The language from some of the very best coaches and leaders I met over the years, captures this notion perfectly. From the lived world of professional sport, I heard these very serious, motivated, focused, and dedicated individuals, tell athletes to, "*go and play with a smile on your face!*" I distinctly remember the first time I came across this, sitting with the staff in one of the most famous changing rooms in world football. Indeed, even more incredible, it was the final thing said by the head coach before the players went out into the tunnel, minutes before kick-off. I recall thinking I would never forget this moment, and would tell all who would listen that even at the highest levels of sport, there was a deep understanding that we are at our best, perform at the highest level we can, when we play, and do so with enjoyment and freedom. This of course did not mean to do just anything, and ignore all rules, and tactics. After all, when children play, they often follow a very strict adherence to the rules and constraints of their games. And we may also note in relation to this, what research has confirmed, that where no external rules exist, children make up their own, and follow these even more closely than anything imposed from without.

Likewise, with professional athletes, I noticed that the tactical and technical demands they had discussed with me when looking at the psychological aspects of their role, were followed most strongly where these contained their own interpretation of what they needed to do to meet their goals. It has long been known in the world beyond the research labs and academia that when we do things for reasons of intrinsic motivation, our commitment to succeed is always much stronger than where we are controlled by extrinsic rewards. This might throw some light on the apparently superficial request to ask players to play with a smile on their faces. What I believe was being said, and was understood by everyone since all had been children at one stage of their lives, was to go out and in front of thousands in the arena, and millions watching on television, and try to play in a childlike way. And to play will always mean with joy and freedom, and sometimes it might even mean with a smile! I think the leaders did not expect players to perform literally with a smile, although some of the best I saw actually did smile, and even laugh on occasions, during performances. I think the staff intended for this to be understood more metaphorically. What they really meant, was to play with an inward feeling of freedom and joy, to allow them to act naturally and spontaneously, trusting more in themselves, and in their abilities, skills, and experience. In other words, to play without fear, based on the belief they possessed the necessary attributes to do well to perform at the level needed, and with a little luck, maybe to win.

There is another idea, associated with playing with greater freedom, which is more profound and challenging in practice. I noticed that the staff and athletes who embodied this notion to the fullest were often those with a particular identity. They were made up of males and females, of all ages, from widely differing cultures, races, ethnicities, and countries. In my work with them, I noticed that they usually possessed a very clear philosophy that guided their lives and work. This could be described as being about, means and ends.

The question of means and ends is a very old one in the history of philosophy, and in very basic terms, is about the ultimate question about meaning, and the purpose of human life. In stark terms, it is, as the famous, or some might say infamous French writer and existential philosopher Jean-Paul Sartre said, about whether life is absurd, or not. His view was that there was no meaning to life except the meaning a person gives it; the alternative and totally opposite view found in existential psychology and philosophy, is that life already has meaning, and our task is to find it. At a more basic level this question, the existential question all human persons face, is really about death. Is death final, or is there some kind of life beyond death?

Now, I must say straight away that although I did hear some of my clients discuss these weighty matters in sessions, this was quite a rare occurrence. When it did take place was where persons were facing career ending situations, when family and friends experienced serious illness, or during other major life situations and challenges. Beyond this, however, I noticed that there was a very powerful correlation between those who told me that their identity was grounded in some form of spiritual, or religious world view, and their ability to perform and play with freedom. In our dialogue, I would explore this relationship to understand how this helped the person from a psychological perspective. It seemed that having an identity whose core was grounded in something beyond themselves, something, or someone whose love and care for them was unconditional, was described by some as truly liberating. One person expressed this vividly by stating, *"it's easy not to hold myself back, to go for it, be free out there and play my game fully, when you know someone has got your back always, even if things go badly!"* If these accounts were coming from good level, committed sports people, then this would be impressive, and worthy of further study. In reality, most of the time these ideas were voiced by highly paid, serious, focused, and dedicated athletes, who performed under considerable pressure, alongside the best in the world.

My summary of what I came across with this group of people, was that maybe we can only play, and really play fully and freely, in the most demanding of arenas, if we are able to keep our performances, and what we do, in perspective. Or to say this another way, the spirit of play can still be found in those who love what they do, but do not allow it to fully define who they are, and their whole lives.

I noticed that those staff and players I worked with who had restricted themselves to what they did, to see everything through the lens of their work, were largely unable to allow themselves to play with freedom. And as Josef Pieper has warned, this attitude has elevated something noble and essential like work, to become everything, and all. I am convinced, that the result of this, is that some people are destined to live half-lives, never able to play, to play freely, and experience deep joy, and happiness, unless it is brought directly by the rewards of their own efforts. And as we all know, often we don't get the external rewards we hope for.

In the end, when everything is seen through the prism of work, we appear more like slaves than free people, and can be controlled and coerced so much more easily.

This brings to mind a final point, that staff often asked me why these people who had greater capacity to play more freely, were so mentally strong. By this term I think they meant resilient, and capable of independent thought; or as existential psychology might express it, happy to accept isolation from others if necessary, and be prepared to think critically. My answer was that such persons had a core philosophy, acquired in different ways throughout their lives, but which allowed them to hold two apparently opposite views together. They believed that everything they did, in and outside of sport, mattered deeply and had meaning, and equally, that ultimate meaning existed beyond the tasks they faced in their lives. And it was in holding both of these views together, albeit that sometimes one might be more dominant than the other, which allowed them to lose themselves in play as they did as young children, even during the most stressful, anxiety inducing, and pressured of situations.

Part II
Major existential themes

6 Identity and meaning

The topic of identity is one that has been much discussed in recent years. Barely a day goes by without some mention of identity politics, identity transformation, and national identity. Politicians, the media, and assorted others, seem obsessed with questions around identity. The famous psychologist Carl Jung felt that questions around identity and meaning were of the utmost importance to everyone. He warned that we were increasingly in danger by shrinking our personal and spiritual identities, highlighting that, *contemporary man is blind to the fact that, with all his rationality and efficiency, he is possessed by "powers" that are beyond his control. His gods and demons have not disappeared at all; they have merely got new names. They keep him on the run with restlessness, vague apprehensions, psychological complications, an insatiable need for pills, alcohol, tobacco, food-and, above all, a large array of neuroses.* As has been explained in the introduction, my focus is exclusively on the importance of identity from a psychological point of view. More specifically, I plan to examine the way in which identity is formed, what role does the individual person have in this process, and what are the implications for organisations and cultures. This book is primarily about performance, psychological well-being, and flourishing, and therefore, it will be important to look more closely at the relationship between these concepts and identity. Lastly, I believe that the topic of identity in professional sport is sometimes easier to come across beyond academic literature. For example, in speaking about what golf means to him, American golfer, world number one, and winner of the 2024 Masters, Scottie Scheffler, mentioned the importance of his Catholic faith in relation to his identity as a professional athlete. Scheffler claimed that, *golf doesn't define me too much……I'm here to compete and do my best…..it's a huge part of my life….I'm a faithful guy and believe in a creator……this defines me the most….I've been given a talent, it's not anything I've done …my faith defines me the most.*

First, I would like to look at how identity affects performance, and conversely, what is the effect of performance on identity. Likewise, in what way does identity relate to the psychological health of an individual person, and how is identity formed through the sport experience?

In his important, albeit succinct review, of how existential psychology had contributed to humanistic psychology, Maslow (1968a) claimed existential writers had made a significant contribution by emphasising questions around identity represent some of the most important that persons ever face. Adopting a holistic position, most strands of existential psychology define identity as being made up of social, emotional, psychological, and spiritual elements. Again, unlike most other approaches in psychology (with the exception of positive psychology), existential accounts strongly emphasise each individual's own active role in choosing and developing their unique identity. When I remember first coming across this idea, I immediately thought that high level sports people in particular would respond favourably to a description of identity where their own input was considered as the most influential part. During the many years of applied practice across a wide range of sports and with performers from a variety of national, racial, ethnic, religious, and cultural backgrounds, I found that in general, the higher the achievement level, the more supportive they were of the notion that who, and what they were, was largely of their own making.

One of the most interesting features, was how my clients would often tell me, that their identity had developed most fully during moments of great adversity. Our natural reaction to hardship and suffering is usually to see these as unfortunate events to be avoided, and most definitely not as something we would choose. I don't think I am overstating the case to say that we feel that instances of great difficulty and adverse situation are forced upon us, or at least, are the result of unfortunate circumstances, or bad luck. In my dialogue with elite level professional performers, I frequently heard something quite different. Although not deliberately trying to make things unnecessarily hard for themselves, a very common theme was that they often chose to expose themselves to exceptionally demanding and arduous situations or events, believing that the psychological and spiritual benefits from passing through these moments (successfully or not), would be of huge importance to them. My reflections on the psychology involved here were that these individuals were knowingly trying to develop their identities (character) by freely choosing the hardest path, rather than alternatives which looked easier, or demanded less.

In recent times there have been many words written about resilience, how to create this in people, and what psychological benefits will accrue. I often come away, from listening to what I am sure are well-intentioned efforts at explaining what resilience is, and how to develop it, thinking that the most important part has been ignored or missed. There are many examples of where people have to find the resources to successfully navigate through difficult times and challenges. Especially after prolonged exposure to hard times, where little seems positive, or even hopeful, it would seem rational and logical to think that these experiences would automatically develop resilient individual identities. The truth of the matter is nearly always the opposite of this. Adversity and very uncomfortable conditions, if imposed on people without their assent, may produce a resilient response during the crisis itself, but this often disappears with the return to normality. This finding is consistent with existential psychology which emphasises that it is the reflection, choosing, and resulting action of the individual themselves, which can permanently change identity. It seemed in so many of the stories of my clients that they had deliberately chosen the less easy way time and time again, and that the lessons learned along the way were more powerfully assimilated because they "owned" these lessons in a way they could never do if they had been thrust upon them.

In the extract which follows, involving a session with one of my clients, I have tried to capture how this type of identity formation process might take place. It was common for these types of encounters to take place at what existential psychologists refer to as *boundary situations*. This term refers to moments when our identities are confronted with a radically new way of thinking and acting. Examples from a sporting context could be, moving to a new club, losing your place in the first team squad, being sold against your will, relocating to a different country, or more personal matters like getting married, having children, experiencing severe illness, or major financial changes. In brief, these *boundary situations* could be described as being either positive or negative, appear to be of great magnitude or not, and be centred on things that don't happen, as much as things that do. The most important point is that the individual person perceives these moments as being very important to their own identity. As can be seen in the example, when facing these moments, it is no easy task to choose a course of action, and therefore dialogue may appear to have a kind of circular quality to it. This should not be seen as a weakness, or failing, but is more in keeping with what Buber (1958) described as a form of I Thou communication. In brief, the I Thou concept describes those moments when we approach the other purely as a person, without thoughts about who, or what they are. In other words, this form of communication is direct, and exclusively focused on listening and responding to the other person in order to have an encounter with them as they really are, and not who we think they might be, based on their past histories, roles, or positions.

Vignette: encounter with meaning

I remember the phone call well. We had worked together for about eight years or so, and during this time the athlete had achieved success at the world level and became a well-known person in the media. I think the journalists liked this person because they were that unusual combination of someone who was polite and courteous, and yet prepared to offer challenging views on a range of matters. Early in their career they tended to restrict themselves to talking about sport-related matters, but as time went on, it became clear that they wanted to express views on a wide range of non-sport issues that were important to them. The call was especially hard for them to do because it was about the very serious illness of a close family member. This was all the more difficult because the ill person was previously an incredibly fit and healthy individual, and was a vital part of the athlete's support team. Unfortunately, the prognosis was very poor, and after a relatively short period of time, tragically, the person died.

Although the athlete knew that my focus was on performance as a sport psychologist, they also understood that my more holistic way of working meant that we would often look at the the athlete's broader life as well as the demands of the sport. As a courageous and resilient person who had learned over a long career to deal so well with the stresses, frustrations and disappointments of professional sport, I felt sure that they would find it easier than most people to deal with this sad and unexpected event. In one way this assessment was correct; the athlete, in the short term, turned their attention to supporting others who had been affected by the bereavement, and after a few weeks, they seemed to have returned fully to their training and competitive programme. But this time something had changed. On the call they asked what my views were on death, what was its purpose, and what might it mean for human beings that all persons will experience this state.

We decided that it was best to meet in person, and at a suitable venue, where we would feel comfortable to engage in what might turn out to be quite an intense and fraught dialogue. I had prepared a few notes and ideas in case these might help with the discussion during our encounter, but as it turned out, these were not at all necessary. The athlete had been doing some thinking about existential topics, and trying to answer the question about whether life, and therefore death, can have any meaning for us, and what that might be. These thoughts had prompted them to do some reading around the topic, which had had the effect of stimulating even more questions. Our work over the next two years became quite different to what we looked at when we first met. It seemed that the death in the family, awful though it was personally, had challenged the athlete to think deeply about the meaning of life, and also about what was the value and purpose of what they did as a professional sports performer. After much discussion they felt that what they did professionally needed to be about life meaning for them; this was followed by a period of intense reflection and reading. This was described by the person as being an uncomfortable and anxious experience, but also one that was liberating, and to their surprise they said, brought a sense of calm and even peace.

The athlete talked about how this experience had made them reflect on their own mortality and the inevitability of death. Rather than leaving them feeling in despair, they described how these thoughts had helped them to see the purpose and meaning behind their own life more deeply. Without any prompting from me, the athlete spoke about how they could now see that what they were doing was a type of personal calling, something they felt compelled to do to fulfil themselves, at this stage in their life at least. I had recently, with a close colleague, Professor Noora Ronkainen, from the University of Bern, finally been successful at getting an article published in an academic journal on the concept of vocation in sport, and so I was very open to what the athlete was now describing. During later sessions we would address the topic of vocation again, especially after the athlete had read psychiatrist and psychologist Viktor Frankl's book, Man's search for meaning, and his approach of Logo-therapy. At this moment, however, she was keen to stress that the death of her relative had made her reassess in a very profound and moving way, exactly how she wanted to carry out her vocation in professional sport, and in her own words, "live more focused on how she did her work, and the influence this might have on others, and less on external achievements and accolades". In this way, I believe she was infusing new meaning into her professional sport existence, one more aware of the importance of values and the type of person she wanted to be, rather than someone only concerned with immediate success. And although this was not the direct aim or goal of our work together, several of the support staff noticed how different this person had become since the death. In summary, she had developed into a much more intensely engaged athlete, but with a greater capacity to be a relaxed, composed, and joyful person. In my view, but more crucially, in the perception of the athlete, these positive changes occurred largely as a result of being able to view her sport participation in a new way, something meaningful in and of itself, and yet with the potential to be an inspirational force of good for others, both within and beyond the world of sport.

Identity and performance

Just before we look at the next example, I would like to say something about the connection between identity and performance. For some time now, there has been considerable doubt expressed about the idea that identity affects performance, and that inevitably, performance will affect identity. There are many reasons behind this state of affairs but I would like to highlight two I feel are most problematic. First, despite there being so much talk about the importance of holistic perspectives, almost all approaches in psychology are grounded in a reductionist philosophy. Reductionism contends that the best way to understand something or someone is to isolate parts from the whole, so they can be studied separately, and therefore, quantified, measured, and causal relations identified. And whilst there is some merit in this, a major problem for psychology is that we end up looking at individual factors detached from a unified whole, and fatally assume that the combination of these factors represents all that we are. In practical terms, the problem that arises from this is that words like love, courage, spirit, self, sacrifice, and happiness, which are not quantifiable, are ignored or denied existence. The devastating result of this is that the individual constructed by reductionist psychology doesn't look or appear to be like an ordinary human person; in fact, it might be closer to reality to say they appear more like a robot, or product of artificial intelligence.

My second issue is around the idea of free will or agency. For quite some time it has felt as though psychology would rather embrace the discipline of sociology instead of re-establishing its roots with philosophy. If we look at the concept of identity, much of what we come across gives the impression that the individual person has very little, if any say, in the matter of who they become, and what they are. The sociological bent in psychology makes it clear that environment is everything; since according to this view we are merely the result of external forces acting on us, words like free will, freedom and personal agency, are viewed as meaningless terms used in less enlightened, irrational and unscientific times. The result of this denial of human freedom has many implications in areas like education, politics, human rights, and law amongst others. In terms of personal identity, it has the effect of treating people as mere categories, whose thoughts, feelings, decisions, and choices are believed to be the outcome of whichever group they come from.

In my work I came across many exceptionally talented people who rejected this extreme collectivist mentality. Whilst acknowledging the help (or hindrance) they had benefitted from in their environment, they knew that the person they were, and their performances, was something they had chosen. These individuals accepted that they had responsibility for the choices they made, and felt guilt when these were wrong or unhelpful, and pride when good or beneficial. In this way, there was an acceptance that each person has a large say in the formation of their identity, and how this interacts with success or failure in their performances. It also allowed them to see that in accepting the holistic idea that we are persons, what took place in their professional lives as sports performers was affected by their broader life, which in turn was influenced sports performance. It seemed to me that the only people I came across in my career who could not see this relationship, or refused to accept it, were some of my colleagues in sport psychology. A stance, I believe, that owes more to their unacknowledged commitment to the apparent purity of reductionist psychology, instead of reality, and the real.

Vignette: finding your identity

This might seem a very strange topic to discuss with a high level professional athlete, given that their role is usually described in very clear and simple ways. To become and remain a professional sport performer is ultimately dependent upon getting results and performing well in their chosen sport. As the saying goes, results and winning are everything; who and what you are to achieve this is of no concern! In my experience, this is a great misunderstanding. The athlete who may or may not produce the desired results, is nevertheless a person, someone whose identity is made up of their sporting role, and who they are outside of this. Over the years, I did meet staff and athletes whose personal identity had almost been subsumed completely in their professional roles. Although some highly talented individuals were able to successfully operate within these narrow and limited identities, they were the exception rather than the rule. And in many cases, they suffered the consequences from this. For example, they often found it impossible to leave professional sport when their time was up, or became addicted to unhealthy pursuits as a way to try to manage the intense performance stress experienced over a lengthy period of time. In contrast, more psychologically and spiritually healthy persons, those whose relationship with their profession was more constructive, were able to do what appeared to be two things in opposition. They could commit themselves fully and with intensity to all that their professional role demanded, and still maintain the capacity to be a person in their own right beyond their sporting identity. During a very exciting moment for an individual athlete I was working with, the importance of keeping the person and the athlete in balance became very evident. After a highly successful phase of the season, both in terms of performances and results, the athlete told me that they had become afraid that their recent success was beginning to consume their whole life. During our dialogue, they told me that previous experiences had led them to believe that this single minded, unidimensional focus, would ultimately prove unsuccessful for their psychological and spiritual well-being, and ability to maintain high levels of performance over a long duration. In great detail, the athlete described how at an earlier stage of their career, they had, in their own words, "reduced myself to being just my results". Out of their passion for the sport and motivation to achieve their goals, they had, largely, unknowingly, shrunken their life and lost themselves totally as a person. And then the inevitable happened. Creativity, spontaneity, joy, and passion were lost, and they began to feel just like a cog in a machine. Relationships with their family, friends and engagement with their broader life diminished, which amongst other things, meant that all they thought about day and night was their next event, and the hoped for results. In addition, this process meant that they lost some of the most important support in their life, outside of sport. These key people also helped the athletes to place their sporting successes and inevitable failures, into a wider perspective, which had allowed them to remember that although hugely important, their professional achievements could not constitute a whole and healthy life. What was exceptionally interesting in this case, was that this athlete discussed the importance of rediscovering a more balanced, holistic, and healthy identity, just at the moment that they were experiencing some of the most outstanding successes in their career. In terms of how they would carry this activity out, we discussed a number of immediate actions, and more longer term developments. Some of the tasks were about small but important matters, such as cutting back on social media, reconnecting to friends beyond the sport, and building back commitments to family. From a longer term perspective, we looked at ideas around pursuing a formal education course, making time for more reading and study, and throwing themselves more fully into a charity project they had always wanted to establish.

As can be seen in this example, much of what takes place in relation to maintaining and building a healthy broader identity, to allow for human flourishing and sustained high level performance, is not about artificially creating some kind of radically new identity. Rather, the task is more often to go back, to renew and reintegrate some of what was done before, and to recommit to becoming a particular person. Very often in dialogue with professional athletes and staff around the topic of identity, the idea of stripping back, instead of adding on new projects, or activities, was a constant theme. Following the holistic ideas of existential psychology and other personalist approaches, the psychological reality, especially for those working in intense performance focussed cultures, was that very often, the demands of the sport tended to narrow a person's identity. Inevitably, the result of this would be that one part of the person had the effect of suffocating the other important, and essential, qualities of that individual. Very often, this process would lead to what Buber (1958) warned about many years ago; the emergence of, *"someone with a stunted person centre"* (p. 25). From a psychological point of view, this narrow and restricted identity is impossible to maintain, and in many cases over time, it will lead to stress-related problems, and even burn out.

Existential identities

Doing well, or at least thinking positively about a performance, tends not to be the most important influence on identity. In contrast, when things have gone badly, or problems have occurred in performance situations, it is at these moments where personal identity can be most affected. I saw on many occasions, that those who were invariably the best at dealing with poor or disappointing performances, possessed a particular type of identity. It is important to mention that these individuals were found across all sports, and were not restricted to a particular social class, age, race, ethnicity, or sex. However, there were some shared qualities which I detected time and again in these people, and how this helped them deal with performance issues was further evidence of the inextricable relationship between performance and identity.

One of the most important topics was around the question of meaning. During encounters with high level athletes and coaches, it became apparent that personality type, or psychological skills, like the ability to focus, maintain confidence or manage stress, was not the key element in how performance challenges were dealt with. I found that the strongest feature was personal identity. These leaders, athletes, and staff talked about their identity being grounded in something permanent, which was described as being largely impervious to what happened in their performances. This is not to suggest that these people were not unhappy, frustrated, or even dejected at times by failure, but that they were quickly able to view these setbacks, no matter how significant, against more important matters. Maybe the best way to illustrate this is by drawing in some real examples of what they said.

One client, after a very brutal and difficult season for her, explained that knowing they were loved and respected by their family for who they were, beyond their sport achievements, allowed them to maintain some motivation, and more importantly, a measure of hope for their future. On an another occasion, a highly experienced and expert practitioner who had lost their job several times at different clubs over a short period of time, discussed how their spiritual and religious belief allowed them to see these difficult moments as being part of their destiny. They stated that despite the psychological pain and suffering this brought, it had the important effect of reminding them that *they were not their job*, no matter how much they loved it, or valued the work.

I do not of course mean that in these two examples feelings of despair, anxiety, and doubt, did not take place. Given the love they had for their occupations, and that both saw them as more of a vocation than a career or job, it was inevitable that there would be great psychological and spiritual discomfort when things did not turn out as they wished. However, it seemed that having the psychological benefit of believing in something greater than one's self, helped these types of people make sense of very difficult times, and adverse conditions.

Psychiatrist and existential writer Viktor Frankl, is often credited as the first person to highlight the importance of finding a broader and deeper meaning in our lives. His most famous book, Man's Search for Meaning (1963), recounts the terrible experience he endured in the Nazi concentration camps during the Second World War. As a medical doctor and someone with psychological training, he observed that those who lived through the horrors of camp life were not usually the strongest physically, or had youth as an advantage, but instead possessed sources of meaning beyond themselves. For some, this was about devotion to a supra-national cause, such as peace and harmony, whilst for others this took the form of spiritual and religious patterns of belief. In his later work, many years after the war, Frankl often said that many of the psychological disturbances, illnesses, and neuroses he came across in his patients, were very often due to a lack of meaning in their lives. The result of his reflections and clinical practice was the foundation of an approach he termed Logo-therapy. In brief, Logo-therapy emphasises the importance to an individual's psychological health and flourishing, in finding a source of meaning which is greater than one's own life and every day existence. Within existential approaches, and in some other traditions in psychology and philosophy, writers have pointed out that the search for meaning is essential to spiritual and psychological health, and that meaninglessness is often at the source of anguish, severe depression, and neurotic anxiety.

Although the persons I worked with rarely encountered circumstances which involved this type of existential threat, or anything remotely like the evil encountered in concentration camps, they did come across moments of their lives when something they loved deeply became unobtainable, or was removed from them. Dialogue during such moments could often be highly emotional and fraught with tension. From an external perspective, this might appear to be a strange affair, because after all, I am talking about individuals who were very often in excellent health, were well rewarded financially, and lived comfortable lives, materially speaking. Nevertheless, this did not preclude them from suffering great personal distress. In order to achieve in any domain, and maintain excellence and outstanding performance, a person must fully commit themselves to the task in hand. An unfortunate, and for some inevitable, side effect of this requirement, is that a person's identity can begin to merge completely with what they do, with their role, or occupation. The result can be very damaging when what you do becomes who you are, because nothing is permanent.

In one sense, my clients were very fortunate, in that they had frequent reminders about the psychological and spiritual peril of narrowing their lives to fit their jobs. Being dropped from the team, injured, replaced by others, transferred, deselected, and other similar ruptures, was the lived experience of performance athletes, and their support staff. It is no exaggeration to say that those, who by design or default, had allowed their identity to be exclusively grounded in their professional role, often struggled to deal with these inevitable critical moments, or boundary situations. Dialogue with individuals during these moments was usually very uncomfortable, however from a more positive perspective, these types of existential *crisis* confronted the person with some clear, but hard choices. Through our encounters and discussion, these persons could see that much of their demotivation, anger, frustration, and anxiety, was related to their failure to maintain and develop a broader identity, one where their professional role was only a part, albeit a hugely important part, of who they were. As can be seen from the examples in this chapter, recognition of this empirical fact provided the opportunity, no matter how uncomfortable, to accept that they had taken the wrong turn. This is no easy thing to accept or deal with, not least because it often goes against the dominant message of many high performance cultures. The ultimately destructive, and despairing message of these cultures, is that in order to produce excellence, a person must dedicate and devote themselves totally, and completely, to their role.

From a more practical angle, I did make use of role models, and other individuals I knew or worked alongside, who had developed a rich and complex identity, despite being highly proficient in their professional role. Sometimes these persons had come to an understanding about the value of a broader identity, after their own struggles as a result of holding a narrow and exclusively role focused outlook. Others were more fortunate, and had been formed and educated from an early age to see the importance of building an ever more complex, and multi-dimensional identity. Usually this formation had been through the influence of parents, good schools, coaches, peers, or other family members.

Maintaining client confidentiality and anonymity, I would draw on material from my engagements with this impressive group, or if the situation allowed, ask them to meet the person I was working with to talk about the benefit of developing this type of broader, more complex, and richer identity. It would frequently be possible for me to draw further on their lived accounts, and discuss in dialogue with my client how they could benefit psychologically from following their own path to identity complexity. For example, we would look at the way in which feelings of depression, anxiety, and frustration, could be reduced by acknowledging and understanding that failures and disappointments in professional life did not define a person. Thoughts would turn to other roles an individual had beyond work, and a sense of balance would reassert itself.

Athletes and staff might be reminded that no matter what successes they had, they were still sons or daughters, fathers, mothers, brothers and sisters, and also friends with people who cared about them, irrespective of what they did, or did not achieve. There would be a recognition that it was possible, and in fact essential at the highest levels of performance, for someone to commit fully to a role, without their role becoming fully themselves.

This apparently paradoxical concept, that is, *being totally engaged but not engaged totally*, can be explained, at one level at least, in terms of time. What is actually being said here is that for psychological and spiritual health, flourishing, and best performances, there has to be a moment when we are not dwelling on past mistakes, and future goals. There must be the opportunity to refresh, recover, and recuperate; to escape from the stress and anxiety associated with your job, occupation, or vocation. The additional benefit is that this is also the best physical, psychological, emotional, and spiritual way to prepare for a task. We refer to this as relaxation or rest, and so it is, but it also helps build our energies for when we resume playing, performing, and working.

Spiritual identities

Some persons might choose to work on achieving a richer, more expansive, and complex identity, through pursuing new interests or hobbies, by returning to past activities, or ways of living. This may sound a rather straightforward exercise, but in reality it can be quite difficult to carry out. One of the reasons behind this is because it is not uncommon for us to invest more and more of ourselves into what we do as we make progress and have success. It is very easy, especially in some national cultures and professional sport environments, to pick up the message that to become the best you can, more and more effort, time, and dedication, is required. Although there is much to commend in the idea that hard work, focus, and motivation are important, people, especially those who love what they do, can easily become the thing they do, and place too much emphasis on working hard to attain success. The result of this can be psychological and physical burnout, staleness, physical exhaustion, constant tiredness, and problems with sleep.

As persons, our overall health, flourishing, and better and sustained performance, depends on us developing in a holistic way. The task we face is to become, each day of our lives, more fully human; a person made up of mind, body and spirit, and therefore, in need of different kinds of nourishment to satisfy each part. Given this diversity of need, which is the result of us being persons, and therefore simultaneously whole and made up of isolated separate elements, we must choose ideas, activities, interests, and passions that can begin to fulfil these needs. Humanistic and positive psychology have both provided models of holism, which in some ways can be seen as more recent versions of the holistic accounts described initially by existential phenomenological psychology. I believe that following these schools of psychology allows us to see human beings as individuals made up of mind, body, and spirit, and who therefore can never be reduced to mere objects. In addition, each of these schools in psychology, in different ways, emphasise that we possess some measure of free will or freedom to choose how we become who we are. Although I found these ideas very illuminating in my own psychology practice, I later realised that my practice really rested most firmly, on psychological ideas around the concept of the human person. It was towards the final stages of my applied work that I came across a definition of the person which I felt most closely resembled the ideas that had been guiding my own approach. I have provided a short extract from this definition, based on a model of the human person by Titus et al. (2020) towards the end of the introduction. For me, not only did this account make sense at a personal level, but crucially, it helped my work with the client group I dealt with the most at the time, who were first team Premier league footballers. The most important reason behind this was because this definition included ideas about meaning and spirituality, and I had discovered, that for many persons in this group, their religious belief was the most important part of their identity.

Vignette: religious faith as meaning

Sometimes athletes are prepared to talk about a wide range of topics, even during initial assessment meetings. I knew a little about this person, not least because they were a world cup winner and someone highly thought of in the world of professional sport. What I could not anticipate however was the type of response I received to one of my opening questions during our encounter. After explaining my role briefly, the way I liked to work and the issue of confidentiality, we began to look at the psychological challenges the player was currently facing. In describing these, and their hope for the future, the player explained in considerable detail how their psychological skills and personal qualities had allowed them to achieve such a successful career. After twenty minutes or so, the dialogue moved in quite a different direction. The player began to talk about what they considered to be the most important defining characteristic of them as a person, and as an athlete. Initially, this lead to a rather amusing but revealing interaction. In trying to follow what the player was describing, I suggested that this sounded as though they believed that they were trying to fulfil their destiny, which led to discussion about the concept of fate. Clumsily, I rather dismissed fate, explaining that this word was not something usually associated with successful people, because it implies that achievements are completely the result of luck and factors beyond someone's control. I continued to explain that some of the most important psychological work and esteemed philosophers argued that the concept of destiny is associated with human flourishing and optimum performance. Unlike fate, according to this definition, destiny describes where the person must actively choose and participate in their own future. Although luck and external circumstances have a part to play, the most important feature of destiny is how the person responds to the circumstances they face. Fortunately, I was prevented from going any further about the differences between fate and destiny, when the player bluntly interrupted me to point out that I was quite wrong.

> *I am sorry Mark, but I completely disagree with what you have said. The most important part of me, the very heart of who I am and how I try to live as a person and a professional athlete is my faith!*

The confusion, about which we both eventually would laugh at, was to do with my Scottish accent and his pronunciation of faith as a non-English speaker! This matter now resolved, for the next half an hour I listened to someone who had left formal education at 16, speak about why their religious faith was so important to them psychologically and spiritually. Although the ideas were usually expressed in everyday language, their depth and range were quite remarkable. I heard that having a religious faith had served to remind him that all his talents were gifts given to him freely, and that his responsibility was to use them in the best and fullest way possible for himself and others. One example he gave was something I had heard several times from other players

> who came from countries where religious faith and spiritual practices were still very much an accepted part of the culture. In detailing critical moments, that is occasions where a major rupture to personal or professional life takes place, he explained how his faith in God helped him to come through these very difficult challenges. For example, a serious injury resulted in him losing his place in the national team and at his own club. During the dark times when most of the medical experts advised that he consider retiring from the sport, he spoke about how his religious practices, such as praying and attending church services, had sustained and helped him to do all that he could to recover, whilst accepting that he did not know what God's future plan for him would be. Towards the end of the session, the player said that his faith had helped him to maintain hope, even when what he was facing made him feel moments of despair and anxiety. In a remarkable statement, he described how the psychological and spiritual concept of hope was like a hidden force, an energy that seemed capable of driving him forward, even when the destination was difficult or impossible to fully see.

There were many other topics this player mentioned about their religious faith, and its importance to them from a psychological and spiritual perspective. One of the interesting aspects to this experience, was how frequently I came across similar ideas, especially during my work in the multi-national, multi-ethnic, and multi-cultural world of English Premiership Football.

When I have written or spoken at conferences about similar examples to this case, the reaction from many psychologists and sports psychologists has been to reject the validity of ideas around spirituality and religious belief, and question whether it is appropriate for such matters to be discussed by a sports psychologist. I have always felt this to be a deeply flawed position to hold, especially as psychology, sports psychology, and psychologists, constantly claim to be an open, tolerant, and non-judgemental profession.

It is also I believe, the result of adopting a very narrow perspective in relation to the concept of identity, and maybe, of not always taking the views of the persons we work with seriously. At a more basic level, it has always seemed to be a somewhat disrespectful, even condescending attitude to take. I heard many times from professional athletes, about their frustrations with psychologists who refused to allow them to talk about the centrality of religious faith in their identity, whilst promoting views about identity that contravened the athlete's values. Given that identity is such a complex and always personally meaningful term, it is not surprising that these athletes reacted so strongly. It appeared to them, as it did to me, that maybe inadvertently, some psychologists were in effect saying, in time and with sound scientific enlightenment, you will reject the nonsense that is spirituality and religious belief!

The chapter which now follows addresses the concept of authenticity, which is one of the most important topics in existential psychology, and ideas about personhood. It is also something I came across on a regular basis in my work with all athletes and staff in professional sport, but most especially, with those persons who had a leadership role. Although it would have been easy to have included discussion on authenticity and inauthenticity in the chapter on identity and meaning, I believe it is such an important matter, that it deserves to be looked at separately. And as we shall see later, the idea of trying to be more authentic is obviously related to our identity in a myriad of ways. One of the easiest to understand at this point, is that we can really only aim at becoming more authentically ourselves when we know who we are. And knowing who, and what we are, is about identity.

7 Authenticity

When we describe something as being authentic, we usually mean that this is the genuine version, or as we would say in more everyday language, it is the real thing. The idea of being more fully yourself, is captured perfectly in the witty but profound statement attributed to Oscar Wilde: *The true artist is a man who believes absolutely in himself, because he is absolutely himself.* Immediately, even from these rather basic definitions, it is possible to detect a very important feature. Whatever authenticity may mean, and as will be quite clear in this chapter, it can have many more interpretations than we might at first expect, this term conveys the idea that something, or someone, is being themselves. This strange phrase, being themselves, suggests that it is very possible to be the opposite of this. In other words, something, or more usually someone, is quite capable of being not who they really are. The existential therapist Hans Cohn, comments, that since *inauthenticity is our denial of the 'givens' as well as our denial of the freedom to meet them....... that we tend to live inauthentically a great deal of the time.* If this all sounds rather paradoxical, then so it is. I have always been struck by how many of the most empirically sound concepts, that is, those things grounded in real life and the real, appear to us in the form of paradoxical statements. Most of the chapters in this book contain similar examples of the paradoxical, however I believe that authenticity might be one, if not the clearest example, of the paradoxical relationship that underpins many ideas and concepts.

The opposite of authenticity is inauthenticity. Interestingly, where this concept is discussed in the psychological and philosophical literature, by far the greatest attention is directed at examining authenticity. Inauthenticity has tended to receive less attention. I think the explanation about this apparent failure to focus equally on inauthenticity is for two main reasons.

First, the perception is that trying to be authentic is in practice at least, a difficult task to achieve. We will look at why this might be so throughout this chapter, and specifically within a case study example. Second, being authentic is highly valued, both in terms of psychological health and individual performance. The psychological approaches which place great emphasis on the importance of authenticity, do so because they are convinced that this quality is something positive, and of benefit to all human persons. Again, I intend to delve more deeply into this assertion, and include part of a case study to reveal how this can be applied in a practical situation.

DOI: 10.4324/9781032669984-9

Throughout my reading around this topic, and informed during years of applied psychology practice, I have developed a different view to the dominant theoretical perspective with regard to authenticity. Although initially I was attracted to the idea of authenticity because it seemed to be something you would expect to find frequently amongst the very best, my experiences influenced me to see authenticity in a new way. Listening to my clients, and reading some critical perspectives in existential phenomenological psychology and philosophical realism, I began to understand that full authenticity was an aim which could never be an expectation. It seemed to me that the more essential activity, was to help people to become more authentic than they were, rather than to somehow achieving this state permanently. In recognising the more dynamic quality governing the desire for authenticity, I was able to broaden my view and recognise that there are several other key elements that need to be in place to facilitate increased authenticity. I will look at these factors in more detail in this chapter, however it might be useful to identify these briefly at this stage.

I observed that cultural, organisational, and environmental issues could serve to enhance an individual's pursuit of greater authenticity, or conversely, could militate against it. In my applied practice in professional sport, much of my work was focussed on what the sport person could realistically hope to achieve given these external constraints. In situations where I was fortunate enough to work with an organisation's cultural architects, for example, head coaches, performance directors, or CEO's, effort could be directed at removing, or reducing, the negative effects of the culture or environment on the search for greater authenticity.

At an individual level within an encounter, we would typically look at factors more in control of the person themselves, and consider how these hindered, or helped, with the path to more personal authenticity. Very often my clients would lead me to consider both their professional demands, and broader life situations. This type of holistic perspective in relation to dealing with authenticity, was of course completely consistent with an underlying philosophy of practice, which was grounded in a belief that person and performance always affect each other, and as has been discussed before, what happens in an athlete's broader life affects, and is affected by, what happens in their professional role.

Why authenticity

I would like to start this section by drawing directly from my applied experiences in professional sport. I have lost count of how many times I have listened to coaches asking their players and athletes to, *"just be yourself as much as you can"*. It took a few years during the earliest phase of my applied engagements, to recognise exactly what these coaches were looking for. Interestingly, matters became clearer when I carried out individual sessions with players, or coaches, and heard the same thing from them in their unique professional sport environments. This type of dialogue would usually occur when someone felt they were not fulfilling their potential, and in their own words, had lost their way, and tried (and failed) to do things beyond their current technical, physical or psychological capabilities. We will look at this in more detail later in the chapter, however the point I would like to emphasise here, is that an awareness of the importance of authenticity, emerged typically, during dialogue around inauthenticity.

That coaches, athletes, and other staff, valued greater authenticity so highly, was plain to see. The psychological reasons behind this commonly held view might not always have been so well understood. Through extensive reading and reflection on the importance of authenticity, I was introduced to the idea that our best performances and psychological flourishing were more likely to take place when we acted authentically. Literature describes a situation where there is a kind of ongoing struggle between our real selves, and another self we may feel pressured to follow. In psychological terms, when we act authentically there is no gap between what we are capable of, and what we are trying to be, or do. At these moments I would often hear the coaches comment favourably, that it was great to see a player *being themselves again* at training, or in match situations. This strange, even paradoxical statement, often uttered casually, as if it was self-evident about how important it was, described what psychological theory has referred to, as congruence.

Work from depth psychotherapists and personalist psychologists has alluded to the idea that, at least metaphorically, we often exist as though we are made up of two different selves within the same human person. This idea about the duality of the human person, their mind, and even their personality, has a very long history. References to this dualism can be found in the work of Plato, Aristotle, Aquinas, and Descartes. In psychology, the famous individualist, Scottish psychiatrist, and author, RD Laing, wrote a challenging and provocatively titled book, *The* Divided Self (1969), which speaks to this concept. His work, based on years of clinical practice, discusses what this idea of a divided self might mean for the fields of psychotherapy, psychiatry, and the caring professions as a whole. With some subtle differences between these thinkers from antiquity and more recent times, there is a general consensus that human persons are at their best when they possess the knowledge, skills, and courage to know who they really are, and to live this in practice.

Fortunately, for those involved in professional sport, although in truth, this can also be applied to all other areas of life, we become ourselves not by thinking about some abstract idealised notion, but through action and living. In his philosophical and theologically informed book, the Acting Person (1998), which is derived from his PhD, John Paul II expresses this idea in a beautiful and inspiring way. The thesis is that by acting as ourselves, we become the best person we can be for others. In this way, authenticity can be conceived as something equally beneficial to the individual person, and the broader community.

Inauthenticity

Several psychologists have argued that it is easier to understand the concept of authenticity, and why it is so important to human flourishing, by considering the opposite pole, namely inauthenticity. It is worth reiterating that living fully in an authentic way is as impossible as permanently achieving complete authenticity. In practical and very real ways, what counts is how close a person is to being authentic, and conversely, how infrequently they are inauthentic.

If we look a little closer at the concept of inauthenticity, we will see that this represents a psychologically uncomfortable, and suboptimal place, for people to be. When we think or act in an inauthentic way, we are psychologically divided against ourselves. The usual result is that we are unable to harness all of our talents in one direction, and appear distracted, unsure, and lacking self-belief.

For a professional athlete or coach who is suffering from inauthenticity, we will often see inconsistent behaviour resulting from confused thinking. In dialogue with athletes or staff during these moments, I would often hear about frustrations and anxiety in relation to their failure to act independently, and to display their real selves. Sometimes this would spill over into feelings of despair, and even self-disgust. I believe the strength of these feelings was related to an awareness, that their best moments and achievements had most usually taken place when they were thinking, and acting, in a more authentic way. Authenticity is additionally so important, because in certain cultures and environments, there can be many external pressures that tempt people to be more inauthentic.

Again, it is worth noting that one of the criticisms I would often hear about players or staff who were largely inauthentic, was that they were, *hiding in the crowd*, and avoiding personal responsibility for their actions. Interestingly, I would come across this statement more often in team sports, than individual. I interpreted this to mean that coaches, and players, knew that the best way to contribute to the team effort was by being the individual you were meant to be.

In more psychological terms, it is easy to understand how an individual person might deny their real self in an effort to fit in. Social pressure from peers, sometimes in explicit form, or on other occasions through subtle forms of coercion, can often place a great strain on the human person not to think and act authentically. Sometimes, it appears as though the group, the team, or organisation, is fearful of people who strive to be more fully their authentic selves. This can be especially evident with younger athletes, or when a new team member is recruited.

It is quite a normal feature of life in work settings especially, that less experienced persons, or new recruits, can often feel a pressure to conform to what they find in their new surroundings. Although this desire to join and become part of the group is often for positive reasons, it can also have very unfortunate side effects. One of the drawbacks associated with trying to fit in, is that the very unique talents, abilities, and skills the person possesses, can remain hidden, or at least, be less evident. It is very natural, and indeed a constructive quality of human persons that when they join a new venture, they are often highly motivated to contribute fully, and make a positive difference. In a professional sports team setting, it is common to see, especially amongst less experienced athletes, and those with less robust levels of self-belief, that initially at least, it appears as though they are doing all they can to hide their own unique capabilities from the group. Instead of helping the athlete to become established in their new home, this strategy of merging into the broader group can cause great difficulties for the person concerned.

For example, I have worked with support staff and coaches who have expressed their disappointment, and even frustration, when a new recruit, fails to make a mark on the group by bringing their unique selves to the party. During confidential individual psychological sessions, I listened to athletes wrestling with their own awareness of how they were holding themselves back from showing their real selves. The brief vignette included in this chapter, tries to capture how this very challenging, and even potentially dangerous situation can be experienced and resolved. The psychology at work here could very easily be likened to RD Laing's notion of the divided self. The person, for the best of motives, does everything they can to become a good team member. Quite often, they will appear to accept guidance and instructions without any resistance, and will direct their own psychological energy to becoming a compliant, and easy to manage person. The reality is, as has been noted both in sport psychology literature and sports writing more widely, that most exceptional performers do not fit easily, and smoothly into all aspects of a team, or organisation's identity. It is almost a truism, that the best performers focus more intently on being the best they can become, even if this results in some level of conflict with others, or misperceptions about their motives.

I was very lucky that most people I worked with in professional sport knew how psychologically problematic it could be, for both their performance, and personal well-being, if they hid their authentic selves in order to experience an easier entry into the group. For example, during sessions in the early part of a player's time at a particular team, dialogue revealed that there had been moments where the person became more aware about their failure to be, *"the player they were meant to be"*. For example, I would hear athletes talking about situations when they tried to do things in matches, or training, which they knew were not skills they possessed. This might, for example, be a more physical and vociferous player trying to adopt a more technical and controlled approach to their performance, despite this not being their natural strength.

Invariably in top level professional sport, when large sums of money are involved, and high expectations are ever present, patience and a longer term view can be difficult to find. An athlete who has become lost psychologically speaking between not displaying behaviour close to their more authentic self, will quickly find themselves subject to intense and unforgiving scrutiny. At these moments, athletes would talk about a build-up of negative anxiety, and use everyday language to describe their feelings of confusion and doubt. They might be able to describe difficult moments during training, in matches, or interactions with support staff, where they recoiled from displaying who they really were, and took the short term, more comfortable option, of trying to become the player and the person they felt others wanted them to be. This dialogue would be particularly fraught and stressful where a player had been dropped from the team, especially for a prolonged period of time. Additional sources of pressure could now begin to appear. For example, mention might be made about how expensive the player was to recruit, or the work that had been carried out to attract them to the club in the first place.

With more experienced players, or those who possessed strong levels of self-belief, there was always a fair chance that work between the sport psychologist and player could help improve matters. This could take place in the following way.

After what often appeared to be a type of circular reasoning, the player might begin to see more clearly their best performances and psychological flourishing had, with few exceptions, occurred when they tried to think, and act, as authentically as possible. Sometimes, I found that a professional sport person might think that this new found knowledge and understanding would be sufficient to help more authenticity to return by itself, as if by magic! Eventually, the player would finally recognise and accept, that becoming more authentic was something they had to take responsibility for. During these moments, I would reflect on how important the psychological literature was on the concept of the *Will*. Although typically seen as a very dated and unscientific term, the Will has a long history in psychology, and interestingly, is still very close to the notion of will power, a phrase frequently heard in real life. According to this perspective, improvements in becoming more authentic, that is, more fully the person you are and were meant to be, would only happen when the person decided to *will* themselves to change.

What is really being said here is that a person should not rely on things happening by themselves, but must reflect, decide, and put their choices into action. These ideas are of course central to the principles of existential phenomenological psychology, and personalist perspectives, emphasising as they do, that human persons possess free will, and as a result, can make decisions to live, perform and be more completely who, and what they truly are.

Vignette: allowing me to appear

One of the most commonly heard questions from coaches I worked with was about how could we encourage athletes to be themselves on the course, court, at the competitive event, or on the field of play. They understood, usually from their own past lives as athletes themselves, but also from observation and reflection, that the best we can be, is by being who, and what we really are. Now, these same coaches appreciated that no one could be themselves all of the time; the quest was to allow more of who, and what you were, to appear more often.

During sessions with younger professional players especially, we would look carefully at this ideal of greater authenticity. These persons were often very aware that the best coaches tried hard to provide an environment in training to allow athletes to be themselves, and not constantly be trying to become something, or someone else. One session with a very talented young player brought out how complex this idea of greater authenticity could be. I had been working with this person for a short time only, and I knew little about her psychologically speaking. I had seen her train and compete, and it was quite obvious, that she was held in high esteem by the staff and other athletes because of her remarkable ability to produce match winning displays when the team was in trouble. At these desperate moments, she would very often show the best of her physical, technical, and psychological skills and qualities, and become someone that even older and more experienced players would look to for inspiration and guidance. In contrast, when the match was less competitive, or the real or perceived challenge lower, she would make very strange, and at times poor decisions, on the field of play. Sitting in the dug-out besides the coaches, it was easy to hear their frustrations and confusion about what they were witnessing. It seemed that the player shrunk on these occasions, and took on a new identity. Anxious looking, indecisive, and distracted, she appeared to be out of her depth, and sometimes, even ready to leave the field of play.

In our confidential dialogues the player explained that although she had seen and could understand the benefit to being more herself, she needed an external stimulus to help this to happen. When matches were less challenging, she described how she went into her shell, and even said that she felt a bit of a fraud, that is not really good enough for the task ahead. I remember listening to this account, and thinking that the coaching team and other staff would likely have been very surprised to hear her talking about feeling so inadequate. In terms of trying to become more authentic, the most essential feature in this case concerned the athlete being able to accept that this experience would feel quite uncomfortable, and might even in the short term, result in poorer performances and outcomes. Being more authentic is something many people are afraid to pursue because there is less of a hiding place when things go wrong. Essentially it means that you risk to be yourself, which, as the best of psychology and the most eminent of philosophers tell us is the optimum we can be. The corollary of this act, in thought or behaviour, is that we must now accept the responsibility for what we do, and that means both successes, and failures. And it turned out that she was equally afraid of both of these outcomes, and believed that hiding in the group, and not being more herself, was the safest option psychologically speaking. This partly explained why she was so much more herself in the most arduous of situations, because nothing was expected of her, and she could forget about the idea of success or failure. In contrast, during competition against much weaker opponents, where success was expected and failure would be seen as a shock, being more authentic was difficult since she would now personally have to face up to the part she played in any unexpected defeat. Much easier to hide in the group, and try to protect yourself psychologically, through assuming a kind of anonymity. This strategy of course, as she knew only too well, is not the psychological and spiritual stamp of the very best, whoever they are, and wherever they are found!

How authenticity

An interesting feature of building greater authenticity is its relationship to self-knowledge. Understanding who you are, and what is most important to you, and why, are some of the component parts of authenticity. In my work, I found that the most authentic people were those who knew themselves well, well enough to often find self-acceptance, and peace with themselves. These athletes and staff expressed how understanding more about themselves, helped them to have the conviction to be who they really were in all situations, since they had learned that this was all that was necessary. There was a recognition nevertheless, that this was both a very difficult thing to attempt to achieve, and yet easy to carry out in practice. Like many aspects of our psychological life, being more authentic seems to involve something that sounds quite paradoxical; it seems authenticity is sought after but maybe only found by a few, because it comes at a great cost, although that cost can be easily met by any of us.

Another way of looking at this, is it seems that trying to be more authentic does not depend so much on what we do, but is more about what we don't do. Frequently, I would listen to very impressive persons talking about trying to allow their real selves to appear more often. It was as if the most difficult obstacle to reaching greater authenticity was not the actions of someone else, but the restrictions in thought and deed they placed upon themselves. And to make the matter even more confusing and frustrating, these highly successful professional sport persons knew that often they had freely, without obvious pressure, or compunction, denied themselves. *They* had chosen to exist less authentically, instead of embracing themselves in order to achieve greater authenticity.

Ultimately, the psychological and spiritual quality of courage is needed to help develop greater authenticity. This is because courage is required in order to allow for an honest self-appraisal and reflection on the past. The need to look back, but not live in the past, is vital to human flourishing, performance improvement, and psychological and spiritual health. I found the best professional sportsmen and women I worked with were able to carry out this task with a forensic honesty.

Facing yourself, seeing your strengths and weaknesses, and trying to recall who you really are, and what you stand for, is no easy task. Many people seem to spend much of their lives trying to live in the moment, just so they can avoid being confronted by their own selves. This is a great pity, although very understandable. As some of the most insightful scholars have explained, it is only by looking carefully at ourselves, that we have any chance of finding out who we are, so we can try to be that person more often.

Courage is also important to allow a person to bring the future into the present. This task, that of thinking ahead, is also an essential to becoming less inauthentic. I saw many professional sports people wrestle with this idea throughout their lives, and be prepared to accept that it is a never ending task. Knowing that authenticity is not a static concept, or final goal anyone can fully achieve, also takes humility. When we look into our possible future, we inevitably project our real selves into a novel situation. This requires courage and humility since we do not know what the future holds. It is, however, an essential aid to building more authenticity, because it forces us to think carefully and deeply about what we really want to happen, and how we should pursue this.

8 Spirit

Love

There are a number of important words in sport that cannot adequately be accounted for by only using strictly psychological terms and concepts. I have in mind the ideas of courage, spirit, sacrifice, joy, and love. All words in this short list are cited often by athletes, coaches, leaders, and most especially by fans, when talking about sport. I often used to wonder why most approaches in psychology appeared to be so reticent to mention these terms, until I thought about the reductionist, materialist, natural science perspectives of cognitive, behavioural, and trait psychology amongst others. There was no room for these psychological spiritual terms, because these psychological approaches have no place for free will, or human agency.

For example, love, being a word so frequently heard in professional sport, is dismissed by much of academic psychology as really being another name for motivation, usually intrinsic motivation. It is quite laughable really to imagine that the power of love, which is one of the most important ideas in human history, could be shrunk by some academics to mean some kind of drive to action. Many people over the years, and in all sorts of situations, have sacrificed their lives for love, love of country, of community, and of family, for example. To hollow out such a concept to a dry psychological construct is, quite frankly, embarrassing.

Fortunately, there are branches of psychology which are more empirical, that is faithful to reality, and have studied and even carried out research into love. Usually following humanistic, existential, Jungian, or other more personalist approaches in psychology, love has been viewed as a psychological and spiritual quality of human beings, one that sets us apart from other living creatures. That we are capable of love, and its opposite, hate, is testimony to the idea that we have free will, human freedom, that we can use for the best, or worst of things.

I think it is reasonable to describe love as, at the very least, a concept made up of both psychological and spiritual elements. Love of sport, love doing sport, and loving thinking about sport are just some of the phrases I have come across so many times in my applied career.

I have often reflected on the fact that very few would be surprised to hear these types of phrases being used in relation to the arts. The stereotype of the musician who lives totally for their music, the poet or writer who tortures themselves daily in their love of finding the perfect phrase or sentence, and the actor who performs with an intensity of being which can only truly appear as a result of love; all of these examples, and more, from the world of arts, are well known to each of us. It is my contention that sports performers are also capable of a similar type of love, or conversely hate, for what they do, and in this way, I think the unique psychological and spiritual elements of sport, would be better off by being viewed as a very particular form of human artistic endeavour.

Now to return to professional sport, not only did I hear players and staff talk about the love they had for what they were doing, but I also came across persons who claimed they hated sport at this level. The first time I heard this in a confidential dialogue, I remember trying to find out what this actually meant to the person, so we could find a way, if possible, to move past this destructive feeling and thinking. Although this revealed a complicated picture, the athlete rejected any suggestion that hate was not the accurate word to use in relation to their current state. They told me that things had gone well beyond feelings of demotivation, negative anxiety, or even despair, and that now they were consumed by hatred for their current life. Interestingly, during this initial meeting, and most certainly when I looked at notes from subsequent meetings, it was very evident how much this person had formerly loved playing their sport, and spoke about the deep joy they experienced alongside the sacrifices they had made to get to such an elevated level of performance.

This connection between intense love and deep dislike, or hate, was unsurprising to me. I had read about this relationship in the works of Jung, May, and other existential psychologists, and in the philosophical books of Pieper. Of equal importance, this theme was also very apparent in the work of great poets, such as Dante, Shakespeare, Robert Burns, and T. S. Elliot. That this collection of some of the most insightful writers on the human spirit could resonate with the experience of an elite level professional athlete, or member of staff, should not really be a surprise to anyone, except maybe a few psychologists who prefer to exist withdrawn from raw reality in their university labs and offices.

Fortunately, there are psychologists working in sport or doing research who are unafraid to carry out the truly empirical task of dealing with, or studying the concept of spirituality, even if this includes the word, love. I believe that this phenomenon will grow in the future, not least because a younger group of academics and practitioners are themselves becoming aware of the importance of spirituality in their own lives. I have supervised a number of sport psychologists, some with extensive experience in high level professional sport, who are increasingly interested in approaches to psychology that are open to the idea of spirituality. In some cases, this has taken place because the sport psychologist has been searching for personal meaning in their own lives, or they have worked alongside athletes for whom the idea of spirit, religious belief, or spirituality, has taken on a new importance for them. This can happen especially during critical moments, also sometimes known as boundary situations, these being occasions where life changing events are encountered. Such exciting, or shattering moments as we have previously mentioned, have the capacity to throw a new light on the familiar, and possibly to propel the person to see things in a radically new, and different way. At these junctures some people will be encouraged to re-evaluate their lives, and begin to examine what they believe in, how they try to live, and why. I have come across these stories frequently in my applied work with athletes and staff, including with those who had previously been quite sceptical about notions like, love, life purpose, or religious and spiritual systems of belief. As a final word, I think the insights from Carl Jung and Thomas Merton resonate deeply with what I have found in my work within professional sport. Jung has written about what he sees as very worrying developments affecting our psychological health and flourishing. He argued, *modern man does not understand how much his "rationalism" has put him at the mercy of the psychic "underworlds". He has freed himself from "superstition" (or so he believes), but in the process he has lost his spiritual values to a positively dangerous degree. His moral and spiritual tradition has disintegrated, and he is now paying the price for this break up in worldwide disorientation and disintegration. ...As scientific understanding has grown our world has become dehumanised. Man feels himself isolated in the cosmos, because he is no longer involved in nature and has lost his emotional "unconscious identity" with natural phenomena.*

Merton on the other hand, has something to add about the idea of suffering, an experience we all encounter in some form as human beings. He views joy as the key to health and human flourishing, and warns us not to, *look for rest in any pleasure, because you were not created for pleasure; you were created for spiritual joy............ spiritual joy ignores suffering or laughs at it........even exploits it to purify itself of its greatest obstacle, selfishness.*

Creative spirit

The topic of creativity features in the chapters on courage and anxiety, because to be creative, requires that a person takes the risk to step away from the familiar, and conceive of a new way. In my work, I often found that the most creative persons were those more strongly endowed with particular psychological and spiritual qualities. I believe that highly creative sports performers must not be thought of to only mean those who play, or lead, with flair and imagination. It is very possible to talk about creativity being about finding new ways to be constructively destructive, to undermine an opponent's strength or advantages, and help make victory more possible. Creativity really means that the person, or persons involved, grasp their freedom to choose to think or act in a way that is uniquely theirs; it says nothing about how aesthetically pleasing, or beautiful this may be!

I also believe that being creative has also for too long been confused with mere novelty, or doing something new for no real reason, a type of change for changes sake. This is quite clearly not what the great writers of literature, philosophy, and psychology mean by the creative act. In line with this thinking, professional athletes and the most impressive and skilled leaders were usually those with the spiritual psychological quality of humility. Humility is an essential component in creativity. This might seem to be a very strange, or even confusing claim to make. I am proposing this, because to be creative requires, amongst other skills and qualities, that we are humble enough to acknowledge another way is possible, and that by definition, we do not always know fully what we are doing, or how things will end up.

Leadership and spirit

I met many leaders in professional sport who were keen to develop cultures of performance excellence and human flourishing, by trying to engender a particular type of ambience. They wanted to have a place where, as one highly successful leader said, "you could smell the spirit", that hit you as soon as you entered the training ground, something full of energy, positivity, and hope! When the word *hope* was used, I recall thinking about the famous anthem sung by the Liverpool FC fans, You'll Never Walk Alone. Originally from the American musical, Carousel, it contains the spiritual line, "with hope in your hearts". I don't know if this leader knew that hope was a concept that has been written about for centuries by theologians and philosophers, and latterly, even by some psychologists, since it is very obviously a spiritual and psychological word, and one of the most important in human life. One only has to look briefly at a sample of work from some of the most famous names in philosophy and theology, to see how much time has been devoted to the idea of hope. And how, despite its apparent complexity and opaqueness, hope has been described as an antidote to despair, and as a psychological spiritual quality that allows us to look forward for the best, even when it seems we are facing the worst.

The French term, *esprit de corps*, is yet another example of where sport and military worlds connect. Although, I did not come across this term in daily use in professional sport, I did listen to leaders, athletes, and staff, talking about the need to inculcate a particular ethos in their club or team, to help generate a particular atmosphere, one where people would be full of spirit. This can be contrasted with the opposite kinds of environments, according to Soren Kierkegaard. In one of the first ever psychological accounts on anxiety and spirit, he refers to these types of environments as being inhabited by spiritless individuals. He continues, claiming that despite appearances to the contrary, such individuals are not living but merely exist, and who it would be more true to say are actually deceased, dead metaphorically speaking, before their time! Clearly, this is very far from the best spiritually healthy cultures, and is not what would be found in any good professional sports team.

I have seen leaders especially, taking a very active role in forming individual and collective spirit in teams and organisations. This has to be done in a way that is congruent with the idea of human spirit. Spirit is not something that can be taught as such; since it is a holistic quality of a person, it does not depend on the acquisition of set skills, or rational knowledge. Instead, spirit is best formed through learning by example, through role models, creative use of tradition, reflection, and establishing a specific kind of culture. The culture needed would have to be anchored in sound health giving values, that is moral codes and ethical precepts that both provide for individual growth, and personal flourishing, and build a sense of oneness, and genuine community spirit. The best first team environments, youth development programmes, and Academies I saw, went a long way to achieving these types of healthy performance cultures. The places not like this, were often unpleasant damaged environments, where staff and players encountered a destructive spirit, one based on fear, coercion, and self-interest.

Vignette: playing with spirit

One of the head coaches I worked alongside was especially interested in the concept of spirit from a practical point of view. As a former professional player and manager in the sport for many years, they had noticed that the best teams and persons seemed to possess another quality, something that enabled them to achieve exceptional performances, often against the odds. I remember asking the manager about why he felt this psychological quality was so vital, and what he called it. He said that for him, he liked to refer to it as a fighting spirit, and that this was beyond ordinary motivation, desire or belief. To make himself more clear, the manager began to talk about one player and a specific team he felt demonstrated great spirit, and described how this could be seen in their actions, and detected in their words. As an applied psychologist formally schooled in an academic discipline that has largely sought to relegate terms like spirit and spiritual to earlier non-scientific, irrational, and so-called unenlightened times, I wondered aloud if we were in fact speaking about different types of motivation or confidence. To these enquiries I received a rather aggressive and direct reply: Certainly not! What he was talking about, he told me, was spirit, which he explained in his own terms, as being, "the part of the human being that holds all the other parts together".

Later on, I would come across similar ideas expressed in the work of existential phenomenological psychology, Jungian psychology, and the writing of some of the most famous and highly regarded philosophers and theologians in history. It has always seemed quite funny, that a football coach who claimed never to have read a book seriously, and left school at a very early age, had come to the same conclusions as a group of intensely intellectual individuals and scholars. It reminded me once again, that the test of the veracity of a theoretical position or concept, should always be its relation to the lived world, to reality on the ground, and what was usually called common sense, or the truth.

Interestingly, this manager was very concerned about how to grow and develop more spirit in his teams and people he worked with. This was looked at primarily in ways beyond religious spirituality, and focused more on human spirit, that is, our capacity to be, and do more, than the limitations we have as a result of our physical, psychological and emotional make up. An example of this was to use the pre-season period to place athletes and staff in very arduous situations, well outside of their comfort zone, and challenge them to find a way to succeed even when their physical, mental skills, and psychological qualities, were being stretched beyond their normal limits. The idea behind all of this, was to build spirit by preventing people from being able to rely on physical attributes, technical knowledge, or psychological skills, to achieve their goals. Instead, a team or set of individual people were thrown back on themselves, and had to find a reason to persist, and hopefully succeed, when the easier option was to accept defeat, and withdraw from the battle.

Another example I came across, involved younger, and less experienced athletes, and staff. Spirit was inculcated within this group by the use of role models, and by encouraging lots of formal and informal interaction between people, so that spirit could be felt, sensed, and encountered almost in a visceral way. In simple terms, this meant that I witnessed great players (and staff) with spirit, serve as inspiration to others who wanted to emulate this quality in their own personal and professional lives. And poignantly, when these players, or even in some cases, support staff or coaches, moved on, retired, or died, people would seek to keep their spirit alive in the club or team.

This was carried out in a number of ways, although I felt that this was done most powerfully, and in keeping with the concept of spirit, through one particular approach. This was where the memories of how these individuals lived, and the way they achieved success during their time with us, was constantly called to mind. The key part to this in relation to the idea of spirit was that the focus was on how something was carried out, rather than focusing on the outcome alone. And as a result of this action, I was never surprised to hear players and staff talk about those they admired as being not only great performers, but of being the owners of a fighting spirit, a generous spirit, or a humble spirit. It is important to note that this was not explained to represent some kind of elite spiritual list, which was only attainable by a very small, and highly talented group. Fortunately, it was frequently emphasised directly, and more powerfully, by indirect means, that these spiritual and psychological qualities were always talked about as something that anyone could acquire. They were not seen as the preserve of only the most gifted. These ideas have been discussed over the years by writers, scholars, and intellectuals of various sorts. They argue that all people equally, can develop and grow in spirit, by virtue of their status as human persons.

Religious spirituality

Every English Premier League Football Club I worked at employed a chaplain, usually on a part-time basis. These persons usually came from a range of mainstream Christian denominations. In my experience, Methodist pastors tended to be most visible in English professional football, although I also came across many Catholic chaplains in other sports. Sports chaplaincy is a well-established part of several Christian denominations, so much so, that academic books have been written about this subject, and conferences and seminars take place most years.

I worked closely on occasion with club chaplains because of our shared interest in providing support to the whole person. Clubs and governing bodies typically welcomed the involvement of chaplains, viewing them as an important source of pastoral support. I used to say that my role as a sports psychologist differed from the chaplain, because I was equally interested in the person and performance, whereas the chaplain's concern was with the social, psychological, and spiritual health of the athlete, or member of staff. There are other organisations, both in private and public spheres, where one can find this type of chaplaincy. I have come across very active chaplains working in the banking and financial sectors, as well as those attached to public health services. Somewhat paradoxically, chaplaincy appears to be most embedded within the military, and professional sport cultures. I say paradoxically, because we might expect to see such people supporting others, where they potentially face death, and serious injury, as a normal part of their occupation. Sport performers do not usually have to confront this level of danger. I have noted previously, however, that although most professional sports do not subject their participants to the level of mortal danger found in the military, the psychological and spiritual demands faced by each of these groups appears very close. The existence of chaplains in professional sports environments is, I believe, testimony to an awareness that there is a need for pastoral and personal support to be offered to all, irrespective of their own religious or spiritual beliefs. The presence of chaplains was a reminder, a strikingly counter-cultural and visible one, that professional sports people should not be fully defined by their performance, achievements, or failures, since the most important element is to maintain respect for them as persons, over and above anything they may do.

During my individual sessions, I came across athletes and staff who were working with me whilst also being supported by the chaplain. Sometimes this was because they were dealing with family, or relationship issues, such as illness, or the death of a loved one. At other times, individuals might seek out advice from the chaplain on spiritual and religious matters. It was uplifting, if sometimes a little surprising, to see that persons from a variety of religious traditions or none, would often meet with the chaplain when facing difficult moments in their professional and personal lives.

I do recall a rather bizarre session at one of the staff Away days I facilitated in a professional sports club I was involved with. Recognising how important spiritual and religious beliefs were to many of our athletes, a sizeable group of whom were from countries outside of Western Europe, a senior member of staff wondered if we could involve the chaplain more fully in our work to improve results on the field of play! Needless to say, we did not alter the chaplain's pastoral and spiritual role, although more usefully, the staff then engaged in a wide ranging discussion about better ways to provide for the spiritual and religious needs of players and staff. Amongst other smaller initiatives, one outcome from this was to establish a quiet space for prayer, meditation, or spiritual reflection, which was available to all, irrespective of faith, or systems of belief.

The presence of Chaplaincy in professional sport helped me as a psychologist keep in mind that we were dealing with people; in the words of the founding father of modern sports psychology, Rainier Martens (1979), people first, athletes second.

On one occasion, I was even emboldened to suggest that staff should attend a monastery for a spiritual retreat. This involved a full day attendance, carried out in complete silence, to allow people to contemplate and engage in a deeper way with their spiritual selves, religious beliefs, or life meaning.

One of the most exciting experiences in my applied career, was being able to work with so many remarkable athletes and staff who came from countries were religious practice, and forms of spirituality, were still very much part of the culture. Especially during challenging moments, or when facing difficult choices, I would be told by these athletes' time and again, that ultimately they felt psychologically able to face adversity, and meet performance expectations, because of the bulwark provided by their religious faith, or spiritual beliefs. It has always seemed to me that this view was not expressed as though believing in some kind of magic, that good things would happen on their own as it were. Rather, what I heard was athletes and staff accepting that their task was to participate fully, give all that they could to succeed, or do well, but with the knowledge that no matter the outcome, God, or a spiritual life force, would always be there to support them no matter what.

Role models from public life, often from outside of sport, would often be talked about in one to one encounters. It was not uncommon to hear athletes especially, speak about how much they admired and respected other influential people for whom their religious faith and spiritual beliefs were so evidently central to who they were. They would discuss about how these individuals showed courage, empathy, or humility, and how despite the sacrifices they must have made, they seemed to be able to carry themselves with great joy and happiness.

I often found that the staff and leaders in professional sport were much more respectful about the value of possessing a spiritual or religious belief, than I came across during my academic life in the universities. This was particularly apparent when I compared the attitude of many sports psychologists I knew, to what I had come across within the world of professional sport. With some notable exceptions, it seemed as though the much vaunted openness and tolerance of psychologists, and sports psychologists, did not extend to the idea of religion, or even less controversially, to the concept of spirituality. It appeared to me that quite remarkably, given very few could be described as Freudians, they had uncritically accepted his view that religion is a psychological crutch, or in his more colourful words, the opium of the people. More likely their closed minded attitude, and reluctance to acknowledge the importance of religious belief and spirituality in the lives of professional sports people, was shaped by their acceptance of psychology as a reductionist science, grounded in philosophical materialism.

9 Anxiety

Existential and performance anxiety

I have left this chapter to last for two main reasons: one sport related, and the other, connects to the concept of ontology. The philosophical term ontology is concerned with ideas about what makes a human being human; how do we define what it is to be a human person, and what are the fundamental and universal qualities we share as human beings. In more complex language, ontology is the study of *being*, that is, what is it that differentiates us from all other types of living creatures on earth.

According to some of the most thoughtful and careful students of the human condition, a group made up of philosophers, theologians, and yes, even psychologists, one of the especially unique human qualities is our capacity to be anxious. And whilst humans are able to experience anxiety because of our ability to freely project our thoughts to the future, or our past, animals are unable to do this, and therefore, strictly speaking, can only encounter fear and not anxiety per se. So it seems that to be human is to have anxiety. Two of the names most associated with the existential perspective devoted much of their time to the study of anxiety. Soren Kierkegaard is famous for saying, *the greater the anxiety, the greater the person!* Building on this idea, and derived from many years of practice as a therapist, Rollo May talked about the benefits of anxiety. He suggested, *to grow as an individual, one must constantly challenge one's structure of meaning, which is the core of one's existence, and this necessarily causes anxiety. Thus, to be human is to have the urge to expand one's awareness, but to do so causes anxiety. Such anxiety is not only inescapable; it is normal and healthy. However, individuals who decide to conform to values arrived at by others, for example, give up their own personal freedom and the possibility for personal growth by seeking "security" in conformity. Such attempts to escape normal anxiety, which is healthy, result in neurotic anxiety, which is unhealthy.*

All of the concepts discussed so far in the book are therefore inevitably affected by anxiety. If this sounds like overstating the importance of this concept, it may be worth remembering that it was no less than Sigmund Freud, the father of psychotherapy and psychiatry, who held that anxiety was "*the nodal point at which the most various and important questions converge, a riddle whose solution would be bound to throw a flood of light upon our whole mental existence* (Freud, 1991: p. 393)".

The second reason for looking more closely at anxiety is that it is one of the most studied and talked about topics in sport psychology. I believe it has been a central interest in the academic discipline of psychology applied to sport because of two important features. First, we hear many times from athletes, coaches, and others about how anxiety has interfered with performance, most usually in the competitive arena. Anxiety is assumed to negatively affect decision making, attentional focus, confidence, and even motivation. Secondly, this in turn has given huge impetus to research study around the mechanisms by which anxiety can impair performance in competitive sport, and how these negative effects can be reduced, managed, or even removed.

So, it seems, both in a sport context and broader life, anxiety has received a great amount of attention over many years. Given this situation, it might be quite natural to imagine that there is very little left to say about the matter. In this chapter, I hope to begin to show that we have largely overlooked a very different view of anxiety, one that could be helpful in understanding how this psychological experience can be beneficial, and contribute to human flourishing, and performance in sport, and more broadly. To achieve this, I will look at the idea of existential anxiety, how this can emerge in the area of sport performance, and ways in which this concept can be encountered in applied work with professional athletes and support staff.

Anxiety and choice

Existential anxiety, as something grounded in phenomenological psychology, is the term given to anxiety about existence. As a holistic concept, this anxiety simultaneously involves both feelings and thoughts. In other words, and in more familiar psychological terminology, existential anxiety is made up of both a cognitive and an affective element.

Phenomenologically speaking, anxiety is the description of an uneasy feeling that appears when we project our minds to some past events, or the future. In contrast, when we are totally absorbed in the present, or deeply focussing on the task, as happens in the phenomenological state of flow, anxiety is absent. At its root, existential anxiety, according to Rollo May (1977), is really about our awareness that death is inevitable, and in another sense, that all we do will eventually come to an end.

With this description, I hope it is fairly easy to see how this type of anxiety connects to questions about meaning, the ultimate purpose of life, and even ideas about spirituality. Existential psychology claims that this type of anxiety is universal, faced by all people, in every place and throughout time. Usually experienced by the human person as an ever present low level sense of unease, its existence points to a very important ontological feature of human being. Put simply, anxiety could not exist without accepting that human persons are endowed with free will. Some existential writers have referred to this by the concept of *situated freedom*, which acknowledges that although we possess genuine freedom, it is always constrained and influenced by a broader context. This context refers to factors largely outside of our control, such as our genetic inheritance, and environmental and cultural milieu. The most important point as far as this book is concerned, is that anxiety conceived of this way, should not be seen as a weakness in human psychology, or a problem to be solved, because it is the inevitable outcome of one of the most important facets of our personhood, namely the existence of human freedom. Psychologists of some traditions and philosophers, use different names to describe this concept. For example, it has variously been referred to as the human capacity for agency, freewill, and is sometimes used to denote the very notion of the self, itself.

Existential sport anxiety

In my work with professional sports people, I frequently came across descriptions of anxiety that were intimately connected with the idea of choice. Athletes would tell me about the anxiety they were encountering around thoughts about changing their coaching team, retiring from sport, taking an unpopular stand based on their own personal values, and many other possible choices, of both a large and smaller kind. Unlike most other approaches to psychology, the existential perspective accepts that anxiety will not only occur as a reaction to our awareness of human freedom and choice, but in our recognition that personal responsibility is also part of this equation.

Connected to this idea, the neurologist, psychiatrist, and founder of Logotherapy, Viktor Frankl, survivor of three years in Nazi death camps, pointed out that the Statue of Liberty in New York needed a Statue of Responsibility in Los Angeles. This humorous yet serious observation, was intended to highlight that freedom, without some constraint, can descend into licence and pure self-assertion. This can destroy community, and turn people into totally self-centred individuals, rather than persons. Given these ideas, it is quite easy to see that anxiety around choice is always connected to values, even if we are unaware of this. Or to put this another way, our choices reflect our ethical and moral codes, and where we try to deny this empirical reality, we can experience the healthy, but uncomfortable feeling of normal guilt.

Guilt and feeling guilty seem to have gained a bad name in most of psychology. In contrast, the existential tradition suggests that feeling guilty when there is no need is a problem, or can be; not to feel guilty when you should, is a concern. In this way, the normal healthy feeling of guilt, albeit a very uncomfortable experience for the person, can be seen more positively where this helps to bring about some kind of desirable change in thinking, or behaviour (May, 1977).

One of the most distinctive features of existential psychology is that it sees the discomfort faced during the experience of normal anxiety as being a positive sign. Whilst accepting that human beings typically do not enjoy the symptoms of anxiety, such as the confused thinking, a sense of physical and mental arousal, and overall feeling of not being in control, the existential view is that these are unavoidable reactions when we care about something. In my applied work, I would sometimes come across professional sports people, athletes, and staff, who had been working with clinical psychologists ostensibly on difficulties arising from anxiety. Very often, these psychologists had, quite understandably, suggested that the best way to deal with the anxiety was to remove the cause. I can't remember how many letters I saw where the psychologist recommended, in good faith, that the best solution for the person was to either prepare to leave or withdraw immediately from their sport.

These individual athletes, or staff, would invariably inform me that whilst their anxiety was discomforting, they were still passionately committed to their role and professional sport participation, and that withdrawing from this was not a favourable option. Often during these encounters, we would look together at where the person had experienced these types of anxiety before. There was usually a recognition that this experience was unavoidable, and was even a genuine indicator of how much they still loved what they were doing, and therefore how important their choices were in relation to this.

It has to be said that very often there would be types of anxiety that were not viewed as constructive, and as something that could be better managed, or removed altogether. For example, and in keeping with traditional cognitive and behavioural approaches in psychology, people would talk about excessive and debilitating anxiety around specific aspects of sports performance. Sometimes in order to deal with this, mental skills techniques, like visualisation, positive self-talk, or various relaxation and meditation techniques, could be usefully employed. I found that this was often more possible in closed skill sports, or with those who had to execute very complex, technically demanding, and precise tasks.

I often came across staff as well as athletes, who were experiencing anxiety thoughts and feelings which they described as being almost overpowering. These were often challenging and difficult encounters, and I had to take care to check and be able to reassure myself that the person was not suffering from neurotic anxiety. Existential psychology describes neurotic anxiety as involving a reaction which is disproportionate to the threat. Neurotic anxiety has the potential to overcome the person, and typically results in them doing anything they can to avoid even more anxiety. The problem though with this strategy is that all choices are accompanied by some level of anxiety, and so the suffering person will tend to try to reduce the feelings of anxiety by restricting their own actions and choices. For example, a person might experience anxiety when they think about changing coaches. To reduce these uncomfortable thoughts and feelings, the athlete might tell themselves that they have no influence over this decision, and deny themselves the possibility of choice. But this can come at a great cost for them. Giving their freedom away, that is by denying their own freedom to choose, and avoiding the responsibility to deal with this, might initially help to reduce anxiety, but the result in the longer term is that the person is now even less prepared to face anything that might cause anxiety. In such cases, it is not uncommon to find that the person withdraws from everything and anything that could potentially involve them in the act of choosing. This can even extend to thinking, where to avoid anxiety, people can be prepared to hand over their freedom to think to others.

We can see this in authoritarian regimes, or where political correctness is prevalent. The result is that critical thinking and the ability to question the dominant groups in society disappears, but as it does, in a cruel twist of fate, the individual person and communities become even more anxious, and keen to conform to the established view. I have seen this happen in professional sports teams, and with a wide range of individuals in sport.

Maybe this is less surprising, since arguably, such a regression has been happening increasingly throughout much of Western society. I believe that this has, quite remarkably, been most prevalent in some of our universities. These institutions, according to John Henry Newman's *The idea of the University*, written almost 200 hundred years ago, are meant to represent a *hedged in space* where open, and free exchange of views, and opinions, can take place!

The philosopher Martin Buber, whose seminal work, I and Thou, (1958) has been long admired by many deep thinking scholars and leaders in psychology and psychiatry, has explained something similar to the existential account of neurotic anxiety. He refers to this situation, where the person deliberately reduces their world in order to avoid the discomfort of existential anxiety and normal guilt, in terms relating to the idea of the self. He memorably described people affected by this psychological and spiritual affliction as suffering from, *"a stunted person centre"*. By this phrase he meant that the individual had deliberately shrunk their own self-awareness and self-knowledge in a futile effort to merge into the crowd, and evade the human necessity to think for themselves, and choose their own actions.

Although I did come across people like this in my applied work in professional sport, most usually this was quite a rare occurrence for me given I do not practice in the area of clinical psychology, and severe mental ill health. I did however engage with many athletes and support staff who were, or had been, dealing with subclinical levels of neurotic anxiety resulting from the difficult working conditions they found themselves in. Sometimes, this was because they had become used to just following what everyone else did, or said, and had handed over much of their freedom to think, and act according to their own ideas, to other people around them. This was often the case when thinking for yourself, and expressing your own views, might bring the person into conflict with other important people in their personal, and professional lives.

The nature of existential anxiety is that the best way to make it grow, to become more of a negative influence in someone's life, is to retreat, or hide from it, and to fail to think, and act, as the innately free persons we have been created to be. The solution to this type of anxiety is not to remove the uncomfortable experience, but to live our own lives, to think our own thoughts, feel our own feelings, and choose. This does not of course mean that the choices we face and make do not have practical, ethical, and moral dimensions, not least because as human persons all of our freedoms exist alongside the responsibility we have to others, whether this be in our closest circles, or more broadly. It also does not mean that we cannot listen to advice, or follow the guidance, and insights from others. The key is, that in the end, it is we ourselves, who make the choice and embrace our freedom, despite any anxiety that might ensue.

I hope that from this discussion about the different ways we encounter existential anxiety in our lives, it becomes clear that the most important psychological quality we possess to allow us to successfully face this uncomfortable condition is that of courage. We have already dealt with the concept of courage and its importance in human flourishing, and performance excellence in professional sport in Chapter 2. I would however, like to briefly mention how to form this psychological quality, to help professional sports people deal effectively with normal anxiety, and the often more intense, and potentially debilitating state, of subclinical existential anxiety.

Embracing anxiety

In my applied work with staff and athletes, I discovered that after we had clarified the likely causes behind their anxiety, our attention would turn to how this could be addressed in very practical ways. I am convinced that most, if not all, of the high level performers I have worked with did not want, or expect, anxious feelings and thoughts to be somehow neutralised by a series of psychological interventions, or various types of mental skills techniques. What was more apparent was that these individuals knew from experience that the problem was not the anxiety *per se*, but rather it was more about them having sometimes slowly, or on other occasions, more quickly, relinquished their freedom to act, or think for themselves, for an easier life, and out of tiredness, or due to laziness. As elite level leaders, professional athletes, and staff, most knew that the solution was not about getting rid of anxiety no matter how painful, but that what was required was to think, reflect, choose, make decisions, and act, and that ultimately, only they could do this, no matter how much excellent advice and support they received from other key people.

Typical sources of anxiety facing professional sports persons could be about a range of matters, such as their future in the sport, the level they hoped to achieve, feelings of isolation and loneliness, feeling not good enough, contractual or financial concerns, not playing, relationships with peers or staff, and media pressures and sponsorship opportunities. Alongside these and other narrow performance issues like maintaining high standards, improving technical and physical skills, and ultimately winning, people in high level professional sport, just like the rest of us, have to deal with the challenges, frustrations, and joys, of our broader lives. This meant that discussions about family, relationships, health, even life purpose, meaning, and identity were often part of my work in these settings. Anxiety relating to all of these elements which took place in an individual's personal and professional lives, was an ever present feature of the one to one encounters with my clients. The case vignette that follows, represents a good example of how existential anxiety could be dealt with in a session, where the person had requested a meeting because they were feeling overwhelmed and anxious.

Vignette: healthy existential anxiety and unhelpful performance anxiety

A very experienced and high achieving member of staff asked to meet, as they were experiencing much more intense and frequent feelings of anxiety at work and home.

The staff member was a very competent and highly regarded professional who had been in their position for many years. The specialist role they occupied required outstanding communication skills, advanced technical knowledge, and high levels of self-belief. Because of the responsibilities associated with their position at the club, decisions and actions around competitive events would be subject to extensive scrutiny by other key staff. And it was not uncommon for this to result in some very stressful, challenging, and fractious meetings post-competition.

I was approached by the member of staff to meet at a private location away from the club so they could feel free to speak frankly and fully. Even though my work was always carried out with complete confidentiality, this was quite a normal request to meet off site, since high profile individuals often felt the need to be somewhere where they could feel more relaxed than in my office, or other rooms at the club. After some small talk and reminders about how I approached my work holistically, what that really meant in practice, the issue of confidentiality, and my approach to feedback from the session, the staff member began to speak in a very emotion laden voice, and I noticed tears in their eyes.

I listened attentively to the descriptions they provided about their general frustrations with their role, and more specifically, how anxious they felt even away from competitions and matches. We looked initially at any possible links between their performance and anxiety, but this was largely dismissed as being not the problem. The thoughts and feelings of anxiety were more about what happened to them when they had quieter moments in their job, when their role was about observation and standing aside to allow others to get on with the task in hand. This anxiety was described as an intense experience of feeling as though they should not be uninvolved, silent, and taking a back seat, but on the contrary, that they should be actively engaged in what was taking place, and that this should be in a very clear and visible way. The person talked about how they sensed it felt as though a huge weight was being placed on them, that their movements felt clumsy, breathing shallow, and hands clammy. These symptoms of anxiety are well known, and have been reported in research in sport and other performance settings, and emerge from accounts of clinical practice. Although not pleasant, and even very uncomfortable at times, these symptoms should be viewed as a sign and an indication that a struggle is taking place in the person. The existential psychology view of this type of anxiety is that it is not in itself a problem, especially when it serves to confront the person with the need to understand why this is taking place in particular situations and at specific moments.

With more dialogue and probing, it appeared that the anxiety was associated with questions relating to identity. What this meant in practice, was that the person tended to think and feel that despite knowing that they could not and should not be actively involved at all times, they wanted to be able to do this in order to feel useful, and in their own words, "not be left alone with my own thoughts!" Existential and other similar depth and personalist approaches in psychology would likely see this anxiety positively since it is reminding the person that being at peace with ourselves, comfortable in the silence of our own lives, is a fundamental part of human flourishing, wellbeing and performance success. However, existential perspectives would additionally remind us that total self-acceptance and complete peace with oneself can never be attained by human beings, although developing towards this goal is to be encouraged. The anxiety the staff member was experiencing amounted to a type of rejection of themselves. They realised that over time, in some quite disturbing and unhealthy ways, they had allowed what they did professionally to become who they were as a person. This shift now meant that in their own words,

> *I have deselected myself kind of, I have defined everything in my life by my job, and when I am not doing my job in a visible way to others, but crucially to myself, I feel as though I am not even here at all!*

This anxiety about existence is really about meaning and life's purpose. When everything centres on something, which, no matter how important it may be to the person, will eventually cease and no longer exist, existential anxiety can become very severe. The solution to this is not to work on removing the anxiety itself, but to re-orient our lives to return to, or begin to discover, more permanent sources of meaning and life purpose. Typically, these can involve spiritual ideas like altruism, care for the world and the human family, religious belief, or commitment to some form of philosophical, or political ideal. At a more basic level, expressions of meaning might be seen through charity work in the community, providing love and service for one's family, or pursuing voluntary work with people in need.

I came across these and other examples of meaning and life purpose with many of the best people I worked with in professional sport. Not only was this ethically and morally admirable, but it also helped the person return existential anxiety back to a normal level. When working on seeking meaning beyond their professional role, a member of staff might find that they began to experience less intense anxiety, and that their work performance also improved. In our dialogue, we would agree that this work-related benefit was very likely due to a new perspective about their role, one that helped them to see that although still very much a passion and important to them, it could not ultimately be everything in their lives. In one sense, the person had fallen into the very understandable trap of allowing the job to do something it was unable to do: to give the complete answer to the question of life's meaning and purpose.

In my applied work in high level sport, I frequently came across views similar to the case just discussed. I believe this psychological outlook is quite common in many people who work in highly stressful, anxiety filled, and exciting occupations and roles. It is easy to see how loving what you do and doing what you love, can, if we are not careful, become all that we are, and shut off thoughts about life purpose and existential meaning. The problem with this, as the professional sport staff member found out, is that when we reduce who we are to become merely what we do, anxiety grows, especially in those moments where we feel we are not doing our job properly, or prevented from carrying it out at all. This final phrase is of course additionally related to the issue of post-career challenges, and facing retirement.

I did work with a small group of people over the years, who did all they could to delay, or avoid, facing the end of their careers. Sometimes in my sessions these persons would talk about the existential anxiety they felt even when they thought about the end, and wondered aloud how they would be able to find anything else in their lives to replace what they had been doing in sport. They kept this anxiety at bay by prolonging their stay in sport, but this was often at the expense of developing themselves more holistically, or searching for other less transient things to give meaning to their lives after their careers had ended.

But it *feels* bad

One of the most powerful critiques of humanistic psychology is that it can sometimes give the impression that not to feel positive and upbeat all of the time is a problem. Not only is it seen negatively, but maybe even worse, it is assumed that we can, and should always, do something about this psychological condition. This has been very powerfully described as, "*the tyranny of the positive!*" This describes the situation where the person who does not always feel positive, or finds it hard to change to a permanently positive outlook, is made to feel there is something wrong with them, psychologically speaking.

Now, if we consider anxiety, one of the least controversial things we can say about it, is that feeling anxious, or should I more precisely say, *being anxious*, is not a pleasant experience. I have never come across an athlete or member of staff in professional sport who told me they liked anxiety so much that they wanted me to make them more anxious! I did, as we have already highlighted, listen to people telling me that in certain situations and circumstances they knew anxiety was a good sign, especially when it was felt alongside excitement. I have always thought, that in one way, what was actually being said here amounted to an understanding, an acceptance even, that it is sometimes a positive to experience something which is nevertheless a negative. I also remember back to my earliest studies into existential phenomenological psychology at the University of Alberta, and being genuinely elated to come across an approach that recognised that everything did not have to be about positive feelings and self-actualisation. This resonated with the well-known saying in Latin, *ex malo bonum*, which translates as, out of bad comes good, or more simply, just because we don't like something does not mean it can't be good for us.

This idea opened up a new vista in psychology applied to human flourishing and performance, and helped me critique what appeared to be the now dominant view in Western culture, that if something doesn't *feel* good it must be bad. I have put feel in italics because it is this drift towards the ascendency of feelings over thought, and thinking, which I believe has led to so much confusion in some strands of academic psychology, and sport psychology especially, around the the concept of anxiety. Very luckily for me, I spent a large part of my professional life beyond the university, engaging with elite level sports performers who viewed anxiety in a much more nuanced, and balanced way.

There were several reasons behind my decision to study the concept of anxiety as part of my PhD research. Performance anxiety was one of the most popular topics in the sport psychology literature during the 1970s, 1980s, and 1990s. The majority of this work was based on cognitive psychology, and most usually described anxiety as having a negative relationship with performance. Although I knew about this perspective, I had been lucky to come across existential phenomenological psychology during postgraduate studies in Canada, and had therefore been exposed to a very different view of anxiety. As we have seen in this chapter, existential anxiety, although understood as something that can produce uncomfortable feelings, is nevertheless viewed positively in certain situations. In addition to this more academic rationale, an important motive behind my interest in the existential account of anxiety also came about because of how the athletes I had worked with experienced anxiety in their lives as professional athletes. The following vignette looks more closely at what it means to like anxiety.

Vignette: but I like being anxious!

We had only begun our work together very recently, and the focus had been mostly on how to maintain a consistently high level of performance across the season, especially at a new and higher standard of competition. During our dialogue, the athlete began to talk about the feelings of anxiety that they were experiencing during the early part of the season. I probed deeper to clarify what they felt were the causes behind the anxiety, and asked whether it was interfering with performance. In very precise and clear terms, the athlete dismissed the possibility that this type of anxiety could explain some of their poorer performances. She said that the hard data available to her in relation to physical output, technical deficiencies, and poor tactics, provided quite enough information to explain why she was struggling at this level. She said that this was not something she was worried about because it was supported by solid evidence, and were things she knew she could improve with the support of her coaches and sports science team. Despite this, she still maintained that much of the time she felt anxious, and interestingly, that this only tended to disappear during actual competition. I asked about other thoughts and feelings she had experienced during this period, and was told that she felt incredibly excited much of the time. She explained this by pointing out that this was the highest level she had ever performed at, and although the jump in standards was quite a challenge, she was elated to have finally made it to this stage. We returned in our dialogue to consider her experience of anxiety again. Drawing on the approach contained within phenomenological psychology, I asked her to describe her thoughts and feelings in as much detail as possible. Anxiety she said, seemed to be ever present, but was accompanied by feelings and thoughts of excitement. According to her description, she felt slightly uneasy at times, and at others she talked about the sensation being like a type of personal disintegration. She mentioned that to counter this, she felt as though she was trying to hold herself together, but that this was only partially successful. In terms of thoughts, she described how she found it difficult to be in the present, to focus completely on the task in hand, and that her mind, as if by its own volition, wandered ahead and imagined what might happen in the future. It seemed as though these thoughts about future outcomes had a life of their own, and in fact, the more she tried to confront her thoughts, the stronger and more embedded they seemed to become. I remember trying to check to see if this type of anxiety was interfering with her daily life and normal patterns of behaviour. When athletes, as they often had done in the past, provided such a rich, complex, and intense account of anxiety, I needed to ensure that we were not looking at a mental ill health issue, and something in need of a referral to a clinical psychologist or psychiatrist. After providing this very detailed description of the anxiety she was encountering, I asked if this was interfering with her sleep, training, relationships and broader life. I was told in no uncertain terms by her, that she expected to have this type of anxiety in the situation she now found herself, and that rather than it being a problem, or something she wanted removing, she viewed it as a good sign. Elaborating on this point, she said that first of all not to feel anxiety like this would worry her. She nicely expressed this by saying that the absence of anxiety in facing this new and exciting challenge for her, would result in her feeling anxious about not being anxious! With little input from my side, the athlete then explained how she had experienced this type of anxiety repeatedly throughout her career, and most especially when she was progressing, and that although it was uncomfortable affectively and cognitively as it were, this was the price she knew she had to pay.

I used this encounter with the athlete as an opportunity to remind her again about the difference between negative performance anxiety, and the much healthier and constructive anxiety inevitably associated with moving on to a higher level. We then talked about how growth, development, and learning can be accompanied by this type of anxiety. She extended the focus of our session to talk about how changing coaches, trying out new approaches to injury rehabilitation, and taking on new responsibilities in her broader personal life, had all been accompanied by anxiety. She began to see that this kind of anxiety is an unavoidable part of making choices, is related to personal freedom and responsibility, and that to experience this throughout your life, as an athlete and a person, is a positive thing, something to be welcomed, despite it not feeling good.

Creative anxiety

In some sports and particular positions on the field of play, as well as within most staff roles, there is a need to innovate and think creatively on occasion. A wonderful small book by existential psychologist Rollo May, called, *The courage to create* (1975), draws attention to the remarkable connections between courage, creativity, and anxiety. In basic terms May explains that since being creative means to think and act beyond existing knowledge or understanding, the person taking this on, is entering into new territory, no matter how small this may be. And what we know about human persons is that before we move into new thoughts and actions, our minds project into the future, and begin to wonder how things will turn out. Will our new way be a success, or might it lead to failure, or worse? And the experience which accompanies these thoughts is what we know as anxiety. It is for this reason that anxiety of this kind has been called the shadow of the creative act.

For the individual person to step into this place of doubt and anxiety requires the human psychological quality of courage. No matter how insignificant, some amount of courage is needed to move beyond the familiar, the well-known, and comfortable.

I saw this take place on many levels in the best professional sport cultures I worked in. In these places, sports science staff, medical personnel, and coaches would be encouraged to think outside of the box, try out different approaches, or challenge each other to come up with new ways of doing things. These performance cultures were riddled with normal existential anxiety, and very often, lots of joy, excitement, and performance success. The leaders in these cultures played a key role in creating the conditions where staff (and athletes) would constantly look for more and better solutions to a variety of problems, and establish a milieu where creative thinking was cherished and welcomed. During recruitment processes, I came across examples of where staff especially were put on the spot, and asked to describe possible new ways of attacking an issue. It seemed that the anxiety created by this approach to selecting staff members was merely a reflection of how the existing staff where expected to behave in their roles. All of these ideas and practices helped make sense of Soren Kierkegaard's famous claim, that anxiety is always the best teacher! Although this phrase is clearly very counter cultural as far as much of the outside world is concerned, it was evidently understood, and received enthusiastically, by many of the most impressive people and organisations I encountered in professional sport.

A broader view

To end this chapter, I would like to say something about the practice of sport itself. Anxiety is built into sport; it is quite impossible to see how it could be otherwise. After all, as the existential psychology perspective contends, most of human life is shot through with anxiety because we are endowed with freedom, the uniquely human capacity to think, feel, and act beyond the influences of our genes, or environment. And as has been pointed out since the time of the ancient Greek and Roman philosophers, human free will is both our crowning glory, and a curse. We are able to use our freedom to participate in our journey towards greater self-knowledge and wisdom, or to deny we possess any agency at all, and hand ourselves over to the diktat of our nature, or to the designs of others.

In sport, especially in individual and highly technical activities, there is much talk about trust. I noticed that my professional golfers and tennis players especially, talked about how key this concept was to excellence, and sustained high performance. It was also mentioned in relation to learning, most vividly when discussing the need to allow a person to trust themselves; such an unusual phrase, and yet one I heard frequently from outstanding professional athletes and staff.

In this context, trust was being used to describe a process involving many psychological elements, from belief and confidence, to self-awareness and focus. In terms of anxiety, I think these athletes were telling me that to trust oneself, to carry out something which by definition is always new, and carried out for the first and indeed only time, involves some experience of anxiety. This anxiety, as we know from our own lived experience, is the result of a combination of the inevitable uncertainty about outcome, coupled with caring about what we are doing. Given this mix, it is impossible not to expect that anxiety will be present. We know that if we have the skills and ability required for the task we face, and also *believe* we possess these, it is highly likely we will perform in that wonderful, anxiety free world, where our own best performances take place, a state we know by the name of Flow. And more profoundly for human flourishing, this holistic personal encounter is where human happiness resides.

During the 1930s and the lead up to world war, the famous English poet, W. H. Auden, exclaimed that mankind was living though a special age of anxiety. By this it seems he was not merely referring to the usual worries associated with the political, economic, and military preparation, for the coming catastrophic events, but that individual human persons were increasingly overcome with excessive anxiety. If it were possible to describe communities and countries as being caught in a type of neurotic anxiety, then we could say this about such a period in history. Auden, and other deep and perceptive thinkers, were aware that people seemed to be prepared to hand over their freedom to anyone, individuals or authorities, who could offer easy and simple answers to life's problems.

Such a tragic situation for humanity reflects the existential idea that anxiety grows if not confronted, and that normal anxiety is the price we pay for being able to think for ourselves, and embrace our innate human freedom. I am convinced that this is not just a problem faced by populations during the interwar years. It seems that doing anything to escape normal anxiety is a constant temptation facing human beings, because we often look for the easy way out, to enjoy a quiet life as it were, even at the expense of denying ourselves the chance to choose another way, one we have decided upon and will be responsible for.

I met so many persons in professional sport who had discerned through their lives that there were many worse things to face than the discomfort of normal anxiety. As we have discussed, they learned these lessons by taking responsibility for their sport, and broader lives, in matters of greater and smaller importance. It was through this path that they found courage was developed, and a stronger commitment to belief rather than confidence occurred. They also began to understand the value of seeking a deeper, more resilient identity, one infused with meaning and purpose beyond sport. And finally, in the title words of Mihalyi Csikszentmihalyi's seminal text, they learned how to go, *beyond boredom and anxiety*, and enter more often into the psychologically and spiritually uplifting experience of flow, where happiness, joy, and optimum performances are found.

10 Paradoxical leadership
Learning from the best

Paradox and the paradoxical have been constant features of my applied experiences in professional sport. I believe many of the most powerful insights are often expressed in the form of paradoxical statements. I am very aware that not everyone will agree with this sentiment, but then, I can comfort myself with what the great Danish thinker Soren Kierkegaard had to say on the matter: *Take away paradox from the thinker and you have a professor!* And despite its note of humour, I am sure he meant this statement to be taken very seriously.

This chapter addresses leadership and culture. I have decided to call my approach by the name of paradoxical leadership, something I hope will sound quite different to some of what we read about in books on management theory and leadership styles. Although this book has not focused on leadership, leaders, whether formally or informally appointed, play an essential role in creating and feeding the culture of an organisation. Leaders are not merely managers, and much less just good administrators, or organisers. Organisational processes and management tasks are of course important, however, a leader is someone who through their character and charisma, in addition to any management skills they possess, is capable of nourishing and guiding the culture.

The qualities and skills necessary to allow for excellence and human flourishing are supported within a particular type of culture. I believe that the best culture is one where a systematic, organised, and rational approach is embedded in an atmosphere of sound ethics, centred on respect for human autonomy, the empowerment of competent people, and driven by care, passion, and spirit. I have written more extensively on practical ways to generate and sustain this type of culture within the context of English Premier League Football in my earlier book, Psychology in Football: Working with elite and professional players. In my experience, many of the principles and practices of exceptional leadership I saw in professional football, rugby, and cricket, were largely applicable across a wide range of sports cultures and organisations. What follows represents very much my own thoughts on excellent leadership. I have coined the term, *Paradoxical leadership*, to capture my thoughts on the best practices I encountered across all my experiences in professional sport.

By the best, I mean specifically those special persons who are able to do two things that many leaders seem incapable of achieving; to simultaneously create the optimum conditions for human flourishing, and for long term performance excellence. It is also important to point out that the term leaders used here refers to those people who are formally nominated to this role, and equally, to the many, often times more influential individuals, who were inspirational and effective leaders without being officially recognised as such by the organisation, or team.

Guided by the spirit of one of my favourite writers, G.K. Chesterton, who was known as the English master of paradox.

Leadership culture

We must be ready to dismantle our successes before they become burdens to be defended. The only time to dwell on your achievements is when you are no longer able to achieve them.

The most important part of diversity in a team is related to ability and skills. But without an agreed set of ethics and a shared morality, it is not a team but a collection of individuals.

The best teams and individuals have an identity; the worst teams are always in search of one or copying someone else's.

Sound performances can lead to good results, but we must beware that often good results can lead to poor performances. This does not mean we should worry about good results, but it does mean that they have the potential to raise expectations, and expectations are dangerous when we expect them to happen!

Everyone knows that too much emphasis on structure can undermine creativity, and too much emphasis on creativity can undermine structure. The real challenge is therefore about how to make this relationship work in practice, especially when half the world hates structure, and the other half hate creativity!

It is often said that the one who least sees themselves as the leader makes the best leader. The problem is that often this type of person is overlooked by other leaders who fear humility, integrity and courage.

Many problems will be encountered when we THINK of a team as being something fixed and permanent, however, even more problems will arise if we don't ACT as though a team were fixed and permanent.

We hear much about the importance of experience, and there is no doubt that experienced individuals can be of great benefit to a team or organisation, so long as what they have learned can help the group rather than hinder it.

The best teams have plans to allow them to be spontaneous ... the worst teams have plans to allow them to be rigid.

Creativity is not about newness per se, but is more about what we do in a unique situation.

The more creative the person or team, the greater the anxiety.

We build resilience always at the individual level first, then the group, and finally the culture.

Culture emerges, organisations are formed, systems are established. The wrong words in the wrong place can cause great confusion....

We value culture not because we can see it but because we can sense it!

Great teams who cohere strongly are always on the verge of disintegration.

You can't have a strong team without congruence on basic values. Values are the cowardly modern world's term for morality and ethics!

Anxiety is the shadow of creativity…creativity always means to leap into the dark, but with a good torch, or the hope of one at least.

Culture is the shadow of the leader….

Culture cannot be measured but it can be felt.

A culture can be destroyed from without, but it is more quickly destroyed from within.

Cultures are like flowers, we tend to think they are unimportant and only about beauty and such trivialities, until we need them.

Take away the vision and you take away the culture. Cultures only grow and thrive where the vision is constantly attended to and nurtured.

Is it possible to care for people as people, and simultaneously care about winning and performing? Er, yes, it's what we are called to do in real life every day….

If your culture puts people first, how will you achieve your goals? On the other hand, if your culture puts achieving your goals first, how will people thrive.

Recruiting good staff is important but changing yourself is more important.

Getting the best staff must mean keeping the best staff you already have.

Systems and structures are essential to long term success as long as they are made to fit the people and not the other way round!

Man management means respecting the human person not as a resource but as an imperfect human being.

To create the conditions where learning is as natural as breathing means we need to focus on the conditions not the breathing!

All human beings possess a human spirit that lets them do things they never imagined they would do in their lives. The key is to feed that spirit with the food it needs – love, respect, autonomy, and responsibility.

Selfish people are often poor at what they do so they blame others: unselfish people are often good at what they do so they blame themselves.

We should not go to a psychologist for answers and solutions, but to learn how to ask better questions and for help in how to confront them.

Psychology is best delivered through other things, and as a last resort, through a psychologist!

Contrary to what is often said, love is not a weak and sentimental thing, but hard, cold and dispassionate. Love requires us to obliterate ourselves for another person or idea, and that is always one of the hardest things for a human being to do.

Without stress we can't function; but with too much stress or too little stress we won't function.

If stress is considered bad, how is that Eustress is the name for positive stress.

The leader should be someone who engenders normal anxiety and excitement in everyone around them, and most especially in themselves.

We want our players and staff to love what they do, but do we recognise that love must always be accompanied by suffering and pain, not only joy and happiness.

Jobs are good, a career is better, but best of all is a vocation.

How do we keep vocations alive and flourishing when the excitement of novelty and the enthusiasm of youth has passed?

People need the basics of life, like organisation and safety, but people without a vision will perish.

The best teams and individuals work towards the common good. The worst teams and individuals only take from the common good.

A team is never just a team of individuals pursuing a common goal, rather, a real team is made up of an individual identity based on a common goal.

The relationship between well-being and performance is so obvious that many refuse to see it.

The best way to improve psychological well-being is by not thinking about it.

We talk more about performance than results because we often don't get what we deserve.

A pure performance focus is never pure, and never only about performance.

Creating the conditions for flow to flourish is the responsibility of the leader; the responsibility of the player is to embrace the conditions fully.

When trust is broken, the best way to regain it is through actions first and actions second!

We must constantly build trust because it can, and always will, fall apart if left unattended.

Trust is not a thing but a relationship, and relationships will always fail even when they appear strong and secure; the message is therefore, how much effort will you direct at maintaining and building trust and what is the best way to do this.

Dialogue is difficult because we have to view the other person as our equal, even if they are not!

Sacrifice is a big word to use about sport, business, education, or any area of life. Sometimes big words are necessary though!

We use the word sacrifice to describe the psychological and spiritual condition when we voluntarily offer all we have and all we can do for the sake of another.

Destructiveness or the desire to destroy something good is never for its own sake, but rather it arises out of a position of weakness and perceived or real personal impotence.

Insecure people, that is, those who feel threatened by the achievements or goodness of others, are a threat to everyone and and especially themselves.

The solution to managing destructively insecure people in an organisation is not to let them into the building in the first place!

Before we can create new ideas and ways of working we need to accept that what was done before must have made sense at the time. This is what it means to build on traditions instead of undermining them.

It is true that fear is a powerful way to encourage others to do things they would rather not do. The problem is that once people get used to doing things because of fear, they forget how to do things for other reasons.

We talk about how a culture of fear can paralyse, but it's truer to say that fear only paralyses independent thought, and that once it takes hold, it is impossible to shift without a bigger fear. Fear begets fear until someone or something breaks the chain.

Aggression is a neutral word like process, transmission, or education, and is always there in some form or another. The task therefore is always about directing this valuable human capacity into something positive and oriented towards the good.

Constructive aggression, to be this, must be grounded in sound ethics and morality. Anything else is mere destructiveness or violence.

Silence can be the most life enhancing word, or the most threatening and fearful. Given this power, it should be used with great care and thought. Unintended silence therefore is a phrase we should never hear in a healthy and flourishing culture.

An organisation without a vision will not survive long. Contrary to popular opinion, dreams are the most practical things we need to guide our actions, because without them, we run the risk of stopping our work when others tell us it is finished.

We talk about organisations or individuals having a great spirit. This can be taken to mean many things, but maybe the most important is that it means that the stronger the threat, the more it grows.

Human spirit is a quality we all possess; the difference is that some people are tempted to deny it because they can't measure it, whilst for others it is because it can't be measured that we know it exists.

The greatest, most highly achieving organisations and people rely on their human spirit to help them surpass their physical and psychological limitations. They do this attending to their spiritual needs through formal, planned, and informal, unplanned methods.

We talk about being able to smell the spirit of a place. The best, smell of a gentle sea breeze, whilst the worst, smell of rotting fish. But fortunately, although we can't create a sea breeze, we can easily throw old fish out!

Love, courage, ethos, esprit de corps: these are the words of the human spirit, and throughout history, they have been the words that have moved the world.

Spirit is never found in the faint hearted, or the mediocre.

For too long play and playfulness have been dismissed as something frivolous and childish. This is a great mistake, since play describes the state when people do something for its own sake, and this is when joy is most strongly felt and our best performances take place.

It has been known for a long time that flow states, where we focus only on the task in hand and consequently perform at our best, arises more often in certain conditions. Organisations which cultivate these will succeed, and those that don't will not.

Flow is not only where we perform our best but where we feel our best. More moments in flow mean more moments of psychological well-being.

Getting into the zone or flow is not only about having the right skills to meet the challenge, but is about believing you have the right sills to meet the challenge. The message from this is that to get more and deeper experiences of flow we need to constantly remind ourselves we have what it takes to succeed.

Flow can be broken in three ways usually. The most common is that the task becomes too difficult for us: next is that we believe the task is too difficult for us: and finally, someone else tells us the task is too difficult for us. The first of these is hard to do much about, in the immediate term at least: the final two are much easier to prevent since they are about thoughts not actions!

Leadership qualities

Being a part is important, but always remember the need to be apart if you want to do your job well.

Trying to be yourself is both the easiest and hardest thing in the world....

For the best performer, their most demanding assessor is very often themselves. Due to this, they need to take care that the assessor is fair and reasonable, not least because they will tend to hear this assessment incessantly!

Who you are is what you do, but really, it's more true to say, what you do, is who you are!

Silence has the power to unlock the most complex of problems, and on other occasions, to block the most simple of solutions.

Real and genuine dialogue is always about more than the words spoken or ideas expressed; it rests on a meeting of minds and hearts, and without a beating heart, a mind would be worthless.

Many high level performers suffer from perfectionism; this is quite unfortunate. However, this is easily remedied. The solution to this affliction, is to ask them to look at themselves in the mirror!

When we say someone has great presence we mean that they are fully focused on the here and now, however, this is only possible because they know who they are, and what they want to achieve.

Please try and be yourself out there, since we recruited you to be you!

Brave persons are easy to find; courageous persons are easy to miss.

People who always look to others for guidance will eventually forget to look to themselves, people who only look to themselves for guidance, will eventually forget to look to others.

Psychological skills are only as good as the person to which they are attached....

Self-knowledge leads to the recognition that knowledge has limits and the self can never be fully known.

A wise leader knows they are always and forever only a steward....

Love asks for nothing in return and as a result it often gets the most back....

Belief is still believing in yourself when you don't feel confident

Confidence is the brittle, nervous, and transient quality that seduces us into thinking we can only perform when it's there...

Players will play for a leader who cares, but they will die for one who loves!

Others may believe in you, but it will be of no avail, or even harmful, if not first accompanied by belief in yourself.

Mental toughness is essentially the capacity to get back up again when the most sensible course of action is to stay down!

Mental toughness is not taught, learned or acquired…no, it can only be bought with the currency of sacrifice and suffering.

The most mentally tough players are often those who are most driven to meet the standards of the harshest of critics… themselves!

To meditate means to allow the mind to rest in one thought; to contemplate means to allow the mind to rest in all thought.

Aiming to be perfect is good, and to be encouraged: expecting to be perfect is bad and never ends well!

Humility is something we all admire in others but are too proud to try ourselves.

A role model is just that, a model. On the other hand, a hero is just that, a doer of heroic deeds. That's because heroes are made of flesh and blood, and models are often plastic!

Thinking for yourself often costs, but not to think for yourself leads to bankruptcy.

Autonomy without responsibility is a fancy way of saying me me me!

To learn from failure really means to keep failure in perspective…therefore the real problem is if we lose perspective.

Encouraging autonomy by giving people responsibility sounds easy until it's your autonomy you're giving up!

To increase our creativity we need to leave space, do little, think and feel less, but act more.

Wisdom begins where self-knowledge ends….

Resilience means to have enough flexibility not to be broken by shocks to the system, and enough core strength not to be broken by the system.

The best psychology practice mirrors life – messy, unfinished, complex, and frustrating, but always hopeful.

Building relationships in performance psychology does not mean becoming friends, but it does mean seeing the other as a fellow human being, not a client, patient, or subject.

Passion is something we expect in all top performers, but the truth is it can't be taught but must be there already. This begs the question about how it got there in the first place.

Love and obsession are as different from each other psychologically as joy and hate. Obsession is always rooted in control: in contrast, love can only be love if it is oriented to freedom.

The best leaders are always the most paradoxical. They are proud but full of humility, lack confidence but possess iron self-belief, have an eye for detail but are never lost in the detail, love people but crave privacy, are deeply generous but stridently parsimonious, and can be incredibly ruthless and remarkably altruistic.

Leaders must have a vision and the vision must be unreal, otherwise what is the point of inspiration!

Skills are learned and abilities are inherited, but more important than these is how they are used, and no matter how we pretend otherwise, that task can only be done by the person themselves.

Bravery is common place – it means to do the right thing without thinking. Courage is more rare – it means to think and still attempt the right thing.

The best perform in the zone often, but the very best often perform when not in the zone.

Ken Ravizza said the zone was overrated, and he was so very right. But Ken was too good a psychologist to use words loosely. His intention was not to deny the importance of the zone, but to remind us that we still can and must deliver on our more ordinary days.

The best get more flow more often. Sometimes this is because they have a particular personality type or possess certain psychological skills, but more often it's because they love what they are doing and doing what they love!

If getting in the zone happens when we lose ourselves in the task, then we need to lose ourselves often in all we do.

Mental skills like good goal setting and imagery can help us to get more flow, but to get even more flow we must love what we do, and love is not a mental skill!

Love means to live in pure self-forgetfulness and yet to feel more alive than ever. It is the state when the thinking mind gives way to the feeling mind. It is where all great achievements in art, literature, science, sport, and business take place.

Passion can lead us astray and distract us from our goals; however, without passion we become lifeless automatons, and no one has ever put their faith in something that's dead!

People confuse motivation and passion. This is very unfortunate since motivation is about our drive towards something, whereas passion is about suffering to achieve something. And it is for this reason that passion is loved by all who deal in excellence, whilst motivation is only admired.

Passion is from the Latin, *passio*, which means to suffer, and to suffer willingly with love. No wonder it is a word that frightens the mediocre and inspires the best!

The most conformist people are those with the strongest beliefs; the problem is those beliefs are usually not their own!

When we talk about the importance of critical thinking we are being academically pompous. Actually, what we really mean is thinking. And this simple word is not so simple in practice, because it requires us to simultaneously listen to others whilst thinking for ourselves!

The vision of the leader is something that must be shared to have any influence; however, the power of the vision rests on the personal commitment of the leader. And therefore, the vision must be nothing less than the life philosophy of the leader – anything less is not worth following.

We sometimes talk about feeling depressed when we actually mean, disappointed. Disappointment is unavoidable, and therefore should not depress us. In fact, not to feel disappointed at some failure or other could be a sign that we are actually depressed!

Existential psychology talks about healthy guilt, and feelings of unhealthy or neurotic guilt. Healthy guilt has the potential to be constructive because it is a recognition that we have failed and can change for the better. Unhealthy guilt, is when we would rather nurse feelings of guilt about something we are not guilty of.

Physical and mental exhaustion can become problems when they are our normal state of affairs. The key is in being able to step back before this point. Sometimes the best person to make this happen is someone else.

Many players play some of the time, some play more of the time, but the best play when they work!

A leader must provide a culture where work can be enjoyed like play. This needs other people to find moments of play even in the most demanding of situations. This will be easier than it sounds though, since anything can be experienced as play, as play describes a state of mind, not an external action.

We say that children play as a way to understand the world. The real challenge is to allow adults to play to understand themselves.

Postscript

I would like to end this book with what might be considered an unusual request, especially given that this work has dealt with applied psychology, and lessons from doing practical work in professional sport environments. It is well known that good theory should make good practice, and the claim that something is right only in theory is often used, quite correctly, to point out that the main purpose of theorising is to improve matters in the real world, the concrete situation as it were. Nevertheless, theory and ideas are eminently helpful if they are used to test ideas, and estimate how things might turn out in practice. And because of this, and that as a culture we increasingly seem more pressured to deliver everything faster than before, and at purportedly higher standards, it becomes even more important that we take time to study and reflect on our options, and choices, to increase the likelihood that these will lead to the best outcomes.

I would therefore encourage anyone who has picked up this book to read some of the literature upon which most of this work rests. The books and articles I recommend are of course personally meaningful to me; they have been my inspiration and guide throughout large parts of the last 40 plus years. They have not been chosen randomly in a haphazard way. This body of work has informed much of my teaching throughout my university career, and provided a source for inspiration and direction for my applied work in professional sport.

Possessing an academic background in both psychology and sport psychology, my initial search involved literature in both of these disciplines. Over the years, I often found that many journal articles and research studies invariably had little to offer, with a few notable exceptions. The most interesting, even surprising discovery, was that so many of the journal articles I found stimulating, challenging, and helpful were written many years ago, or appeared in fairly obscure publications. My experience has been, that much of what appears in scientific journals in sport psychology, either lacks ecological validity, that is, it is not grounded sufficiently in the reality of the real world of professional sport, or focuses on topics of minor concern. Apart from these drawbacks, there is another I have encountered, which is most certainly not the preserve of sport psychology academic literature, since it is an accusation that has been levelled against all academic areas. It is the tendency that exists to repeat the same ideas, to study the same topics, and be guided by the same theoretical perspectives.

I know I am not alone in being someone who increasingly stopped carefully reading content published in the traditional journals in my field, and instead looked beyond this work, especially to books and chapters written by the original authors. Following this method led me to the works of Maslow, Jung, Van Kaam, May, Frankl, Maritain, Buber, and my most influential guide, the combined works of Josef Pieper. These writers, most of whom were either psychologists or philosophers, addressed the topics I was coming across in my applied work, despite not one of them apparently having ever delivered psychology in professional sport, or written directly about this type of human activity. It was through this literature that I also learned more about the perspectives of Plato, Socrates, Aristotle, Aquinas, and Lao Tzu. This was complimented by reading the poets, Pope, Dante, TS Elliot, Burns, Shakespeare and others of this fame, as well as drawing on specific books like Newman's Idea of a University, CS Lewis' The Abolition of Man, Boswell's Life of Dr Johnson, and Tolkien's Lord of the Rings. This corpus of work, literary, poetic, philosophical, spiritual, and psychological, turned out to be of far greater value to me than almost all of my reading in sport psychology. The exception would be the original and ever-stimulating literature by Csikszentmihalyi on flow, optimum performance, and happiness, Deci and Ryan's organismic cognitive psychology work on self-determination and intrinsic motivation, and articles by Professor Ken Ravizza, now sadly deceased, on sport psychology, self-awareness, self-knowledge, existential themes, and what he called, the zone.

What was remarkable, and exciting, was how material from this incredibly diverse group of writers and academics, made so much more sense in relation to what I was dealing with as an applied psychologist working with persons in high level professional sport, than did most of the body of literature called sport psychology.

Finally, I hope that in the years ahead, a new generation of sport psychologists will find ways to broaden their reading, and study carefully those who write about real practice with sport persons. Even more important, they will be courageous enough to seek out, or revisit, the most important theorists and thinkers of psychology, including the pioneers of the discipline, as well as more recent contributors.

In order for this to take place more easily, I believe we will have to do much less research, engage in more critical thinking, and place greater value on reflections from the field. I believe that what is at stake is nothing less than the future of sport psychology, and even much of academic psychology itself. If we continue to produce so much research for the sake of research, whilst ignoring the needs and challenges people face in real life, funding will dry up, and courses will shrivel and die. Resources are under pressure as never before; the competition for who gets what, if anything, is about to get very intense.

But to finish on a more optimistic note, history reveals that in the end, the truth will out! The real, the theoretically fruitful, and practically useful, will grow and flourish; the artificial, the superficial, and purely abstract will perish. It is only a matter of when.

Bibliography

Assagioli, R. (1993). *Psychosynthesis: a manual of principles and techniques*. London: Harper Collins Publishers.
Buber, M. (1958). *I and thou*. New York: Scribner.
Caruso, I.A. (1964). *Existential psychology: from analysis to synthesis*. London: Darton, Longman & Todd.
Chesterton, G.K. (1908). *Orthodoxy*. San Francisco: Ignatius Press.
Cooper, A. (1998). *Playing in the zone: exploring the spiritual dimensions of sports*. Boston: Shambhala Publications.
Corlett, J. (1996a). 'Sophistry, Socrates and sport psychology', *Sport Psychologist, 10*, 84–94.
Corlett, J. (1996b). 'Virtues lost: courage in sport', *Journal of the Philosophy of Sport, 23*, 45–57.
Cowen, A. (2024). *Analytical psychology and sport: epistemology, theory and practice*. New York: Routledge.
Csikszentmihalyi, M. (1975). *Beyond boredom and anxiety*. San Francisco: Jossey-Bass.
Csikszentmihalyi, M. (1992). *Flow: the psychology of happiness*. London: Rider Publications.
Csikszentmihalyi, M., & Csikszentmihalyi, I. (1988). *Optimal experience: psychological studies of flow in consciousness*. Cambridge: Cambridge University Press.
Deci, E.L., & Ryan, R.M. (1985). *Intrinsic motivation and self-determination of human behaviour*. New York: Plenum Press.
Frankl, V.E. (1963). *Man's search for meaning: an introduction to logotherapy*. New York: Pocket.
Freud, S. (1991). *Civilization and its discontents*. New York: W.W. Norton & Company.
Gamble, R., Hill, D.M., & Parker, A. (2013). 'Revs and psychos: role, impact and interaction of sport chaplains and sport psychologists within English premiership soccer', *Journal of Applied Sport Psychology, 25*(2), 249–264.
Giorgi, A. (1970). *Psychology as a human science*. New York: Harper & Row.
Giorgi, A., & Giorgi, B. (2008). Phenomenology, In J.A. Smith (Ed.), *Qualitative psychology: a practical guide to research methods*. London: Sage, 25–52.
Jackson, S.A., & Csikszentmihalyi, M. (1999). *Flow in sports*. Champaign, IL: Human Kinetics.
John Paul II. (1998). *Fides et ratio*. Boston: Pauline Books.
Jung, C.G. (1956). *Two essays on analytical psychology*. New York: Meridian Books.
Jung, C.G. (1964). *Man and his symbols*. London: Dell Publishing.
Jung, C.G. (1995). *Modern man in search of a soul*. London: Routledge.

Kelly, P. (2011). Flow, sport and the spiritual life, In J. Parry, M. Nesti, & N. Watson (Eds.), *Theology, ethics and transcendence in sports*. London: Routledge, 161–177.
Kelly, P. (2023). *Play, sport and spirit*. New York: Paulist Press.
Kierkegaard, S. (1980). *The concept of anxiety*. Princeton, NJ: Princeton University Press.
Kingston, F. (1961). *French existentialism: a Christian critique*. London: Oxford University Press.
Laing, R.D. (1969). *The divided self: an existential study in sanity and madness*. Middlesex: Penguin.
Marcel, G. (1948). *The philosophy of existence*. London: Harvill.
Martens, R. (1979). 'About smocks and jocks', *Journal of Sport Psychology, 1*, 94–99.
Martens, R., Burton, D., Vealey, R.S., Bump, L.A., & Smith, D.E. (1990). The competitive state anxiety inventory – 2, In R. Martens, R. Vealey, & D. Burton (Eds.), *Competitive anxiety in sport*. Champaign, IL: Human Kinetics, 57–72.
Maslow, A.H. (1968a). *Toward a psychology of being*. Princeton, NJ: D. Van Nostrand.
Maslow, A.H. (1968b). What psychology can learn from the existentialists, In A.H. Maslow (Ed.), *Toward a psychology of being*. New York: Van Nostrand, 95.
May, R. (1960). *Existential psychology*. New York: Random House.
May, R. (1975). *The courage to create*. New York: Norton.
May, R. (1977). *The meaning of anxiety*. New York: Ronald Press.
May, R. (1983). *The discovery of being*. New York: Norton.
Merton, T. (1961). *New seeds of contemplation*. New York: New Directions Publishing Company.
Murphy, R., & White, T. (1995). *In the zone: transcendent experiences in sport*. New York: Penguin/Arcana.
Nesti, M. (2004). *Existential psychology and sport: theory and application*. London: Routledge.
Nesti, M. (2007a). Players and persons, In J. Parry, S. Robinson, N. Watson, & M. Nesti (Eds.), *Sport and spirituality: an introduction*. London: Routledge, 135–150.
Nesti, M. (2007b). Suffering, sacrifice, sport psychology and the spirit, In J. Parry, S. Robinson, N. Watson, & M. Nesti (Eds.), *Sport and spirituality: an introduction*. London: Routledge, 151–170.
Nesti, M. (2010). *Psychology in football: working with elite and professional players*. London: Routledge.
Novak, M. (1994). *The joy of Sports: endzones, bases, baskets, balls, and the consecration of the American spirit*. Lanham, MD: Madison Books.
Pieper, J. (1963). *Leisure: the basis of culture*. South Bend, IN: St Augustine's Press.
Pieper, J. (1989). *Josef Pieper: an anthology*. San Francisco: Ignatius Press.
Pieper, J. (1995). *Divine madness: Plato's case against secular humanism*. San Francisco: Ignatius Press.
Pieper, J. (1998). *Happiness and contemplation*. South Bend, IN: St Augustine's Press.
Pieper, J. (1999). *In tune with the world: a theory of festivity*. South Bend, IN: St. Augustine's Press.
Ravizza, K. (1977). 'Peak experiences in sport', *Journal of Humanistic Psychology, 17*, 35–40.
Ravizza, K.H. (2002). 'A philosophical construct: a framework for performance enhancement', *International Journal of Sport Psychology, 33*, 4–18.
Ronkainen, N.J., Tikkanen, O., Littlewood, M., & Nesti, M.S. (2015). 'An existential perspective on meaning, spirituality and authenticity in athletic careers', *Qualitative Research in Sport, Exercise and Health, 7*, 253–270.

Ronkainen, N.J., Tikkanen, O.M., & Nesti, M.S. (2018). 'Vocation: a concept for studying meaningful lives and careers in sport', *International Journal of Sport and Psychology, 48*, 1–100.

Schall, J.V. (2012). *On the unseriousness of human affairs*. Delaware: ISI Books.

Seligman, M.E.P., & Csikszentmihalyi, M. (2000). 'Positive psychology: an introduction', *American Psychologist, 55*, 5–14.

Tillich, P. (1980). *The courage to be*. New Haven & London: Yale University Press.

Titus, C.S., Vitz, P., & Nordling, W.J. (2020). *Theological and philosophical premises for a catholic Christian meta-model of the person*. Arlington, VA: Institute for the Psychological Sciences.

Valle, R.S., & Halling, S. (1989). *Existential-phenomenological perspectives in psychology*. London: Plenum Press.

Van Kaam, A. (1969). *Existential foundations of psychology*. New York: Image.

Vitz, P. (1997). *Psychology as religion: the cult of self-worship*. Grand Rapids, MI: Eerdman.

Watson, N. (2011). Identity in sport: a psychological and theological analysis, In J. Parry, M. Nesti, & N.J. Watson (Eds.), *Theology, ethics and transcendence in sports*. London: Routledge, 107–148.

Index

academic sport psychology 12, 17, 55, 58, 61, 70
acquiring courage 35–37
Acting Person (1998) 97
aggression 128
Allardyce, S. 11
analytical thinking 2
anxiety 2, 10, 11, 19–20, 68, 111–123; choice and 112–113; creative 121–122; embracing 116–119; existential 111–112, 116–118; feels bad 119–121; negative 99; neurotic 114; performance 111–112, 116–118; self-doubt and 27; stress and 36
Aquinas, T. 3, 14, 25, 29, 55, 60–62, 97, 134
Aristotle 3, 14, 25, 29, 55, 97, 134
arousal 54; mental 113; physical 113
arrogance 48, 51–52
artificial intelligence 85
Auden, W.H. 123
authenticity 9, 11, 18–19, 63, 93–102; how 101–102; importance of 97; inauthenticity and 97–101; why 96–97
autonomy 42, 130

behaviourism 8
belief 16–17, 38–52, 129; arrogance 51–52; confidence and 40; excessive self-belief 47–50; perception and 15; practical self-belief 43–46; religious spirituality and 19; self-belief 40–43, 51–52; self-determination 8
Beyond boredom and anxiety (Csikszentmihalyi) 65, 123
Bolton Wanderers 12
Boswell, J. 134
boundary situations 45, 68, 69, 83
bravery 27, 34, 130; courage and 26, 29–30; physical 29, 30, 33; *see also* courage

Buber, M. 83, 88, 115, 134; *I and Thou* 115
Burns, R. 104, 134

caritas 55
Catholic faith 81
chaplaincy 108, 109
character of courage 30–32
Chesterton, G.K. 1, 41, 125
clinical psychology 113, 115
coercion 98; punishments and 66; threats and 47
cognitive psychology 65, 120; de-humanised 8; organismic 8, 134
Cohn, H. 95
collective courage 34
communication 83
compassion: care and 55; ruthless and 48
Competitive Sate Anxiety Inventory (CSAI2) 10
confidentiality 12, 13, 16, 17, 38, 39, 44, 46, 47, 90, 117; belief and 40, 123; feelings of 39; lack of 39; performance 38; self-belief and 41, 42; skill of 39
constructive aggression 128
Corlett, J. 14, 26; *Courage in sport; virtue lost* 26
courage 13, 14, 16, 25–37, 43, 67, 102, 115, 122; acquiring 35–37; athlete 34–35; bravery and 29–30; character 30–32; collective 34; group 34; humility and 102; mental toughness and 31–32; resilience and 32–35; staff example 28–29
Courage in sport; virtue lost (Corlett) 26
The Courage to Create (May) 27, 121
creative anxiety 121–122
creative spirit 105–106
critical thinking 45, 52, 114, 131

Csikszentmihalyi, M. 17, 48, 64, 65, 72, 123, 134; *Beyond boredom and anxiety* 65, 123
cultures 1, 65; Anglo Saxon 72; environment and 27, 62; flow 66–67; holistic 12; leadership and 124–129; performance 20

Dante 104, 134
Deci, E.L. 8, 134
Descartes 97
destructiveness 127, 128
Devaney, D. 4
dialogue 2, 11, 12, 14, 15, 20, 26, 31, 33, 36, 39, 44, 45, 48–50, 58, 59, 61, 68, 89, 90, 96–99, 101, 104, 127
The Divided Self (1969) 97

Elliot, T.S. 104, 134
embracing anxiety 116–119
emotion 53; passion and 54; subjectivity and 61
English Premier League Football 11, 93, 124
enjoyment 68, 75; happiness and 64; performance and 17; playfulness and 66
ethical codes 4, 31
excessive self-belief 47–50
excitement 19, 20, 68, 126, 127
existential 1, 3, 6, 10, 81, 82; anxiety 19, 36, 118–120, 122; authenticity 18; crisis 90; identities 88–91; performance anxiety and 111–112; phenomenological psychology 1, 3, 9–12, 19, 27; principles of 27; psychology 18, 36, 77, 87, 114, 131; sport anxiety 113–116; threat 89
extrinsic motivation 53, 54

feelings 8; affirmation 40; anxiety 114, 116, 117; competence 40; confidence 39; confusion 99; destructive 104; doubt 99; guilty 113; inadequacy 49; love 61; meaninglessness 18; passion 60; sacrifice 61; self-determination 67
flow 53, 64–77, 123, 127–129, 131; cultures 66–67; finding 70–72; permission to play 74–77; play and 72–74
flow-light condition 69
Forde, M. 11, 12
Frankl, V.E. 84, 89, 113, 134; *Man's Search for Meaning* 84, 89
Freud, S. 26, 111

frustrations 66, 71, 93, 101, 117

genetic inheritance 3
Graham, M. 53
group courage 34
guilt 86, 113, 131

happiness 5, 42; enjoyment and 47; flow play and 17, 64–77; genuine 9; joy and 110, 126; sport and 17
Hawthorne effect 15
Heidegger 25
helpful passion 57–60
holistic 7, 8, 13, 17, 18, 57, 82, 85, 87, 91, 96, 106, 123; culture 12; psychology 59
honesty 3, 5, 102
human freedom 9, 123; awareness of 113; denial of 85; existence of 113
humanistic psychology 9, 42, 81, 119
humility 48–51, 105, 130

I and Thou (Buber) 115
The idea of the University (Newman) 115
identity 12, 45, 59, 77, 99; definition of 82; existential 88–91; finding 86–87; formation 83; meaning and 18, 81–94; performance and 85–88; resilient 123; spiritual 43, 81, 91–94; unconscious 105
imagination 3, 73, 105
inauthenticity 9, 94, 95, 97–101
information technology 8
intrinsic motivation 6, 53, 65, 66, 134

Jackson, S.A. 64
Jung, C.G. 81, 103–105, 107, 134

Kelly, P. 64, 72
Kierkegaard, S. 106, 111, 124

Laing, R.D. 97, 99
Lao Tzu 134
leadership: culture 125–129; paradoxical 20, 124–132; qualities 129–132; spirit and 106–108
Leisure: The basis of culture (Pieper) 3, 61, 72
Lewis, C.S. 134
Littlewood, M. 4
Logo-therapy 84, 89, 113
love 56, 62, 64, 103–105, 128; caritas 55; obsession and 130; passion and 7; self-forgetfulness 131

Maldini, P. 39
Man's Search for Meaning (Frankl) 84, 89
Maritain 134
Martens, R. 10, 20, 109
Maslow, A.H. 9, 18, 42, 81, 134
May, R. 1, 25, 27, 29, 104, 111, 112, 121, 122, 134; *The Courage to Create* 27, 121
meaning 4, 5, 8–10, 40, 69, 76, 77, 118, 123; encounter with 83–85; identity and 18, 81–94; religious faith as 92–93; spirituality and 91
meaninglessness 18, 89
mental exhaustion 132
mental ill health 15, 60, 115
mental skills 13, 27, 69, 131
mental skills training (MST) 11, 13, 69
mental toughness 129, 130; courage and 31–32; resilience and 16, 26
Merton, T. 38, 105
moral decision 29, 32
morality 31; ethics and 4, 14, 33, 59, 126
motivation 62; extrinsic 53, 54, 66; intrinsic 6, 53, 66; passion and 17, 131; principles of 13
motor control 7
MST *see* mental skills training (MST)

Nazi death camps 113
negative anxiety 44, 99
neurotic anxiety 114, 115
Newman, J.H. 38, 115, 134; *The idea of the University* 115
Nietzsche 25

obsession 130
ontology 2, 111
organisational psychology 11
organismic cognitive psychology 8
over confidence 16, 38, 39, 47

paradoxical 44, 61, 95, 97, 102, 109; leadership 20, 124–132
passion 7, 17, 53–63, 130, 131; conceptualisation 60; sporting 55–56; as suffering 56–57
Paul II, J. 97
perceived competence 67
performance 3, 12, 16, 36, 38, 44, 65, 125; anxiety 41, 116–118; catastrophic 70; confidence 38; culture 20, 90, 106, 122; domains 4; enjoyment and 17; exceptional 16, 72, 107; flow 73;

identity and 81, 85–88; optimum 73, 92, 123; play 73; psychology 3, 6, 12, 13, 47, 130; sports and 14, 59
personality 8, 9, 75; motivation and 7; theory 8
persons 1–3, 6, 9, 12, 34, 45, 50, 60, 73, 85, 87, 91, 105, 113; belief 15; brave 129; communities and 114; courageous 16, 129; flow 66; perception 15; performance and 96; religious spirituality 108, 109; resilience 32; self-belief 40; self-esteem 47; special note on 20–21; sport performers and 13, 59, 100; trust 123
phenomenology 17, 64, 65
philosophical materialism 26
philosophical realism 61, 96
physical bravery 29, 30, 33
physical danger 34
physical exhaustion 132
Pieper, J. 3, 25, 48, 55, 61, 72, 77, 104; *Leisure: The basis of culture* 3, 61, 72
placebo effect 15
Plato 97, 134
play 5, 6, 31, 43; competitive 57; flow 17, 64–77; foul 29; permission to 74–77; spirit of 75
playfulness 66, 73, 75
Pope 134
practical self-belief 43–46
psychological qualities 13, 33, 38, 54, 58, 116
Psychology in Football: Working with elite and professional players 124
psychometrics 31

Ravizza, K. 4, 69, 70, 131, 134
realism 3, 61, 96
reality 1–3, 6, 21, 27, 40, 44, 46, 50, 75, 77, 85, 91, 99, 103, 107; empirical 113; psychological 87; suffering 56
recognition 10, 38, 90, 102, 114, 131; acceptance and 68
reductionism 7, 25, 85
reductionist psychology 85, 86
religious belief 33, 88, 91, 93, 109, 110
religious faith 34, 110; centrality of 93; as meaning 92–93
religious spirituality 19, 108–110
resilience 82, 130; courage and 32–35; mental toughness and 16, 26
Rogers, C. 9
role models 90, 106, 108, 110, 130

Ronkainen, N.J. 84
Ryan, R.M. 8, 134

sacrifice 63, 104, 127; love and 61; passion 58; suffering and 56, 130
Sam, B. 12
Sartre, J.-P. 76
Schall, J.V. 56, 64
Scheffler, S. 81
self-acceptance 102
self-actualisation 9, 42, 119
self-appraisal 102
self-assertion 113
self-awareness 14, 115, 123
self-belief 17, 38–43, 51–52, 98; building 45–46; confidence and 41, 42; excessive 47–50; genuine 51; humility and 48; practical 43–46
self-centeredness 9
self-determination 8, 67, 134
self-disgust 98
self-doubt 27, 50
self-esteem 47
self-expression 63
self-forgetfulness 131
self-fulfilment 55
selfishness 9
self-knowledge 14, 51, 52, 101, 115, 129
self-motivation 53
self-respect 33
Seligman, M.E.P. 47
Sewell, D. 10
Shakespeare 104, 134
Shankly, B. 53
silence 110, 128, 129
situated freedom 112
skill learning 7
social pressure 98
Socrates 134

sound performances 125
spirit 6, 19, 33, 57, 66, 103–110, 126, 128; creative 105–106; identities 91–94; leadership and 106–108; love 103–105; playing 73–75, 77, 107
spirituality 19; *see also* religious spirituality
sporting passions 55–56
sport psychology 2, 3, 6, 7, 10, 14–17, 20, 26, 62, 112, 133
sports chaplaincy 108
sports medicine 12
stress 9, 13, 20, 126; anxiety and 32, 39, 90
suffering 17, 31; passion as 56–57, 62; personal distress 89

Taylor, M. 12
thoughts 8; behaviour and 9, 53; courageous 33; excitement 120; feelings and 8, 114; independent 77, 127; uncomfortable 114
Titus, C.S. 20, 21, 91
Tolkien, J.R.R. 134
trust 12, 42, 123, 127; relationships and 28; self-belief 40, 42

uncomfortable 9, 11, 68, 82, 84, 90, 98, 113–115, 117, 120, 121; emotion 41; thoughts 114
University of Hull (UK) 10

Van Kaam, A. 134

Watson, N. 21
well-being 17; flourishing and 18, 50; mental health and 41; performance and 127; psychological 18, 19, 81, 87, 127, 128; spiritual 87
Wilde, O. 95
Wundt 26